MARRYING OUTSIDE OF GOD'S WILL

FRANCES DUPREE

FRANCES DUPREE

Marrying Outside Of God's Will

                     Copyright (c) 2020 Frances Dupree

All rights reserved

The characters and events in this book portrayed are a part of my life story and character names have been created. Any similarities to real persons, living or dead, is not mentioned to intentionally place in any way harm.

No part of this book may be reproduced, or stores, in a retrieval system, or transmitted in any form or by any means, electronic, mechanical or photocopying recording or otherwise, without prior or written permission of the author or publisher.

Printed in the United States of America

"This book is dedicated to all those I hurt in the process of finding me."

Frances Dupree

INTRODUCTION

∼

God told me not to marry him, but if he was going to marry anyone it should be me. I stayed with him through the lies, the betrayal, the beatings, the cheating, and the threats. I knew I deserved to be a wife. I would soon learn that yes, I deserved to be a wife; but not his wife.

Despite my disobedience God never took his hand off of my life. When the time was right, God connected me with a strong support system that I would need to me get through my roller coaster ride, of a life.

Whenever my spirit was weary God would always come and see about me, whether it was someone calling to check on me, or me running into the right person, or I would go to church and the sermon would be just for me. But God never left me nor did HE forsake me. When the time was right, he gave me the strength to leave.

CHAPTER 1

I was heartbroken. What did I do wrong? Why didn't he love me the way that I loved him? How could he show me pure and genuine love and then turn his feelings off like water? These were my daily thoughts. After reading his letter years later; I would find out that I didn't read the letter the right way.

EVEN THOUGH I WAS COMPLETELY BROKEN ON THE INSIDE, ON THE outside I acted as if there was nothing wrong. I acted as if I was just striving and trying to find my way through life. I couldn't allow what I was feeling and thinking on the inside to show on the outside. This would make me vulnerable and it would give others the opportunity to judge me.

WHEN I WAS ALONE ALL I WOULD DO IS CRY AND SCREAM, FIRST I lost my best friend, lover, provider, and supporter to jail. He was all of that plus so much more to me. Then he writes me and tells me not to wait for him. I was love sick. I was so in love with him that the daily functions in life became a struggle. I no longer had the motivation to drag myself out of bed and go on about my day. I couldn't stand the sight of myself in the mirror.

BUT SOMETHING INSIDE OF ME WOULDN'T ALLOW ME TO GIVE UP. I would say a little prayer and cry out to God every morning and every night. Then I would give myself a little speech all just to get out of the bed. Once I was out of bed the real Frances was left behind. I put on the fake happiness and smiles while all along with every step I took I was dying on the inside.

I WAS ONLY SEVENTEEN AND I KNEW I WOULD NEVER EXPERIENCE love like this again. I felt as though there wasn't even a point in dating or trying, there would never be another him. Our love could never be replaced, the touch of his hands, the way his skin felt on mine, the way he kissed me with so much passion. I couldn't do it without him, to me it wasn't acceptable. He pushed me to my fullest potential, he believed in me when I didn't believe in myself. He saw something in me that I didn't see because when I was frustrated and wanted to give up but he wouldn't allow me to. Giving up wasn't an option no matter what.

THERE WEREN'T ANY WARNING SIGNS SO I DIDN'T SEE THIS coming, I was completely blindsided. This was a pill I couldn't swallow but I didn't have a choice. His mind was made up and I had to learn to live life without him. I didn't even know this was possible. The heartache that I felt to me was worse than death. I had to go on with life alone again without my soul mate. I really wanted to just give up, but I hoped the day would come that he would change his mind and I needed to be at my best because he always pushed me to be my best, and he wouldn't accept anything less from me.

Up until I met my first love, I didn't think it was possible for anyone to truly love me. I grew up in foster homes and group homes. When I was seven years old, I got into trouble and my mom beat me. She would always tell me if I didn't like it that I could leave. Well this was that day, I packed my roller suit case and went next door to my best friend's house. Her mom saw the marks, whelps, and bruises on my arms and legs and called the police. I was taken from my mom that evening and she never was able to get custody back. I didn't meet my dad until I was sixteen and based on the lies that were told to me when I was younger that relationship was destroyed. It was me against the world, at least that is how life was until I met my first love and he loved me unconditionally. He provided for me and supported me through any dreams that I wanted to accomplish.

This is why it was so devastating and my whole world destroyed. Love isn't supposed to be able to be turned off like that. I didn't do anything to cause him to not love me anymore. Was I just unlovable? Was I meant to be in this world alone and heartbroken? Why would God allow me to experience true genuine love and then allow it to be taken away from me? It had to be me, it had to be something about me that I couldn't be loved. First, I was taken from my mom and she didn't get me back, then even though it was my fault the relationship between my dad and I was destroyed, now my soulmate was gone.

CHAPTER 2

I enrolled in CNA School. I heard through the grapevine it would be easy to graduate and in the end of me completing the class I would get a decent paying job. To try and keep my mind off of what was really going on, I fully dedicated myself to school. Not only would I graduate but I would graduate at the top of my class.

A FEW WEEKS IN AND THERE WAS THIS CUTE NERDY GUY IN THE class. I was the new girl getting side eyed by a boy named Timothy. He was taking the class with his sister. He was cute to me in a weird way. He wore glasses and was dark chocolate. But he had the sexiest body. I became study partners with his sister. Eventually I and Timothy also became study partners. Eventually we went from study partners to having a full-on sex-buddy, relationship sort of thing going on.

ALL THIS WAS A DISTRACTION, BECAUSE AS SOON AS I WAS ALONE ALL

I could do was think about my first love. I could hear his voice in my head. My heart was still broken and even though Timothy was slinging the pipe well he could never replace my first love. Even though my body was yearning for sex my heart and soul was still with my first love. We had an understanding and that was sex only.

I DIDN'T WANT A RELATIONSHIP AND NEITHER DID HE. HE WAS love sick over his ex-girlfriend and I was love sick over my first love so the arrangement worked perfectly for the both of us. No strings were attached; we didn't owe each other any explanation. When we wanted sex, I would go over to his house and spend the night, and the following morning in class you would never know that we were sleeping together.

I STILL LIVED WITH MY FIRST LOVE'S MOM. EVEN THOUGH WE weren't together anymore, she and I built our own relationship that had nothing to do with him. Momma Nikki would encourage me to move on and live my life. I just wasn't ready to do that yet. I still had hopes that my first love would change his mind, and if he did, I wanted to be ready and I needed no one to be in the way. It was still hard for me to accept that I had to live life without him.

I GRADUATED, AND I PASSED STATE TESTING AND I BECAME A certified CNA. I was only seventeen and I got my first CNA job at Del Rosa Villa. I was turning eighteen in two months and they were short staffed so the hiring manager told me not to tell anyone my age. I was hired on the spot and I started the next morning. I was so excited, I had to go buy all white scrubs. My excitement faded that fast because I had to go shopping and my first love wasn't with me. Simple things like this, our alone time made me miss him even more.

It felt good that I accomplished my goals. In the back of my mind I knew that my first love would have been proud of me. He would have been the first one by my side to get my state results. When I found out that I passed he would have been telling me I told you that you were gonna pass. But that wasn't going to happen, I had to stop thinking about the past and strive to see what was in store for me in the future. Even though I was heartbroken, and I felt like I couldn't live without him; I had to accept reality.

CHAPTER 3

For a while I was content with going to work and then going home. I was still so sick in love yet slowly but surely it was starting to get a little easier to handle day-by-day. I started eating a little more and I was actually getting some sleep. By this time, he hadn't written me any more letters so it was obvious that I wasn't a priority to him. I had no other choice but to put on my big girl draws and continue to live my life.

ONE DAY WHEN I WAS WALKING HOME FROM WORK, I GOT LOST and then I met Joshua. He pointed me in the right direction and told me that he lived on nineteen street that if I ever wanted to hang out or get out of the house that was the spot. He seemed cool so one day I went over there. However; on my way walking to his house I met Allison. She seemed cool too. We just started talking and I told her I lived on sunrise. She was telling me how she was dating an older guy, but they kept it a secret because they started dating when she was fifteen. She said that he had approached her, and he didn't care so she didn't either.

FRANCES DUPREE

. . .

One day there were a group of guys playing basketball and that's when I saw him, Levi. He was the finest thing on the block to me but I wasn't the type to approach a guy, so I just looked and never said anything. When I got to Joshua's gate there was a guy sitting there named Tom. I told him I was looking for Joshua, he told someone else and they went looking for him. I sat and talked to Tom for a while.

I told him I had recently moved from Apple Valley and I didn't know anyone. Joshua was the first person I really met since I moved out there. He asked me if I was seeing anyone and as much as it broke my heart I said, "No". I pointed Levi out while he was playing basketball and I told him that I thought he was cute, and he said everyone thought he was cute. We laughed about it and talked about any and everything until Joshua came.

Every time I would get sad and start crying over my first love, I would go to Nineteenth Street and hang out just to keep myself occupied. I didn't realize it but I stopped giving myself prep talks and praying in the morning. Instead I was more focused on going to hang out. One time I had to go to the bathroom and I told Joshua that I was going to go home, and he told me I could use the one in his house and that his brother would meet me at the door. I was hesitant, but I agreed.

CHAPTER 4

When I got to the door it was Mr. Handsome himself (Levi). I couldn't help but blush as he took me to the master bedroom, which was his other brother's room. On my way back out of the bathroom I passed his room and he was playing super Mario brothers. He told me to come in and we sat and talked for a while. He wrote his number on a piece of paper and put it in my purse. He told me to call him and I told him not to hold his breath.

I WOULD GO BACK AND FORTH UP THE HILL BECAUSE I WAS ALSO working at a convalescent hospital in Victorville. I was working the night shift and I was having a hard time staying awake. So, I flipped my purse over and went looking for Mr. Handsome's number. I called and when it rang, I hung up before anyone could answer. I called again, and we stayed on the phone talking for hours.

WHILE WE WERE TALKING, HE TOLD ME THAT IT WAS HIS BIRTHDAY

and it was raining. He told me that everyone left him that it was just him and his grandma at home. I felt bad for him and I told him when I came back to San Bernardino that we should hang out and do something for his birthday. Every day we would talk on the phone until I went back down the hill. I realized that I had a crush on him but of course I wasn't going to say anything about it.

When I made it back to San Bernardino, I let him know and he invited me over. I went to his house and hung out with him for a while. He offered me spend the night with him, but I didn't end up staying. Levi would come to my job in San Bernardino and bring me lunch or take me to lunch. He was the hottest thing on the block and he always had a crowd around him. That made me more attracted to him.

He was smart, intelligent, a very hard worker, he didn't smoke or drink, he was staying with his mom to help her with rent and bills. He wasn't anything like my first love, but he caught my attention in a different way. When I was in San Bernardino, I started spending all of my free time with him. I never did well alone, when I was alone reality would set in. The hurt from losing my first love was still there. I was just trying to cover it up. The loneliness and abandonment issues would start to play tricks in my mind. So, I made it a point to try and always be distracted and not alone in some way.

CHAPTER 5

One day my friend Allah and I were hanging outside on sunrise in front of my house. Levi and his brother Jaxon had just left from playing basketball at the school. He hit me up because he made it a point to know where I was at all times. I told him, and that's when they came to chill with us. His brother Jaxon asked my friend what those high desert niggas were like and she told him that she had a boyfriend. Before I could say anything, Levi said that I didn't know because my nigga was right there. I immediately started blushing and didn't know what to say. We were officially dating after that.

I FINALLY STAYED THE NIGHT AT HIS HOUSE. WE WERE IN HIS room chilling and he was playing the game. He asked me if he could taste my lip gloss and I said yes and he kissed me. I thought that was so cute. He tried to have sex with me and I lied and told him I was on my period and I even asked his sister in law for a tampon to play it off. I didn't believe in sleeping with someone on the first night.

. . .

FRANCES DUPREE

When I went home the next day, I felt weird and awkward because I was still living with my first love's mom and I just spent the night with another guy. Momma Nikki, however, told me it was okay. Even though things were okay with her it still didn't sit well with me. Momma Nikki was my mom and I never wanted her to feel disrespected in any way.

I was still commuting up and down the hill for work. But now when I was down the hill I would stay at Levi's house. He cleared out some drawers for me in his room and he said I was with him now and I shouldn't be living with my first loves mom anymore. It was so hard for me to tell her that I was moving out. She was my mom now and his sisters and brothers were my sisters and brothers. Momma Nikki said she wanted me to be happy and that she understood and that I was going to be her daughter no matter what.

Levi helped me take my stuff from her house to his. I felt so guilty, but I was happy at the same time. I was hoping that I found love again. That night Levi's ex-girlfriend called him and he was talking to her on the phone as if I wasn't even there. I got mad and tried to leave but he wouldn't let me. When I thought he was asleep I snuck out and headed back to mom's house. He ran in the alley bare foot and with his clothes on backwards to stop me and have me go back in the house. I thought that was so cute and even though I felt disrespected I went back in the house with him.

My birthday came around and we had plans to go out. But someone had stolen his money out of the closet and he was pissed. He went off this was the first time I really saw him mad.

MARRYING OUTSIDE OF GOD'S WILL

I felt important though because he kept saying he was trying to take his girl out for her birthday and they were fucking things up. We went to eat at Cocos, while we were eating my phone kept going off Momma Nikki and my sisters were calling to tell me happy birthday. This really pissed Levi off.

Levi got mad, hurried up, paid the bill and walked out leaving me sitting there. He was mad because he had told me before that he didn't want me talking to them anymore, but it was hard to just stop, they were my family. When I wasn't around Levi, I would still talk to them, sometimes when he would go to work I would sneak to sunrise and visit. Momma Nikki told me that he was showing signs of being controlling and that I needed to be careful but I didn't listen.

CHAPTER 6

I thought Levi was a knight in shining armor. When he got mad, he was so disrespectful, but everyone had their flaws in my eyes. Levi started getting into it with his mom and brothers a lot it was time for us to get our own place. When we were both off at the same time, we would go apartment hunting. Levi had joined the CCC and he had to go on spike. While he was gone, I was to go to work and to stay in his room. The crazy part is I did exactly what he told me to do. I would go to work, pick up extra shifts because being alone wasn't good and thoughts of my first love would flood my mind. So, I made sure that I stayed so busy that by the time I went to Levi's mom's house all I could do is shower, eat, and pass out.

One night I was asleep and Levi's sister and her friend tried to come in and jump me but his mom saw what they were trying to do and she came in the room right in time and stopped them. I jumped up out of my sleep. I didn't do anything to them so I didn't understand what the problem was. Turns out the sisters' friend liked Levi and that's why they were trying to jump me in my sleep.

THE NEXT DAY I WENT TO MOMMA NIKKI HOUSE AND I WAS telling her and my sisters what happened. Mom told me I needed to be careful and I could always come back home. My sister Kamil wasn't having it and she was on a rampage; she went to Levi's mom house to fight his sister but I wouldn't let her and I begged her to go home. She told me she was going to catch her slipping and she wasn't going to let it slide.

LEVI ALWAYS WAITED UNTIL NINE O ONE TO CALL ME BECAUSE that is when our minutes were free. I missed him while he was gone. I was alone again, something that I didn't want to experience because all I would do is think about my first love. When Levi would call, he would tell me how it was going on spike I especially loved how the raccoons were stealing him and his coworker's food. I would tell him everything about my day. I told Levi his sister and her friend tried to jump me while I was asleep but that his mom walked in right on time. He was pissed and said that he would handle it when he got home.

I WAS STANDING OUTSIDE OF THE GATE IN FRONT OF HIS MOM'S apartment and Allison popped up out of nowhere and asked if I was talking to Levi. It was really weird. I told her yes and to mind her business she said my bad that's my friend. I was so stupid I didn't put two and two together that Levi was her secret boyfriend the whole time but the truth would come out later.

I TOLD LEVI AND HE SAID NOT TO PAY ALLISON ANY ATTENTION

that she was just a fast ass little girl on the block always in niggas faces. He changed the subject quickly and told me how much he missed me and he couldn't wait to get home. But he wouldn't tell me the exact day he was coming home.

When Levi got home, I was so excited. I missed him a lot, and now I didn't have to worry about being alone anymore. He checked his sister and her friend real quick too. As for he and I; we had the best sex that night. I don't know if it was because I hadn't had none in a while because I didn't remember it being that good before and right after I rubbed his back. He told me he loved me for that because no other girl ever did that for him. I would iron his clothes and tie up his boots on his way to work in the morning. I was in love all over again but it wasn't anything like the first time.

CHAPTER 7

*L*evi and I started looking for our own place. Things were getting weird at his mom's house. He and his family were starting to fight a lot. One day I was at work and Levi called me on my break. He said that he and his brother Joshua had just got into an argument and I asked him why and he said because of me. He asked me if I was ever dating his brother and I told him no. I told him I met his brother first but it was never like that. That I thought he was just coo as Hell. He said that his brother liked me and was getting on his head because he felt like he stepped on his toes and I told him I never knew that, and I didn't even get that kind of vibe from him.

AFTER THIS WHEN I WOULD SEE JOSHUA IT WAS AWKWARD BECAUSE I didn't even know that he liked me, and I wasn't the type of chick that would go between family members. I mean I had my ratchet moments but that would be beyond ratchet and it wasn't my get down. I never looked at him in that type of way at all. I just always thought he was a coo ass dude and that was as far as it went.

FRANCES DUPREE

. . .

God was always on time, it got to the point where I didn't want to be at Levi's moms anymore. The fighting was beginning to be too much for me. Out of nowhere I got a phone call that we were approved to move in the Victoria Village's. We were so excited about it. He kept saying I did something no one else could do and that was to move him out of his mom's house. Moving day came and my dad came to help us, he even surprised us and paid the full move in.

The ladies in the office liked my dad. They were like putty in his hands. That night Levi threw a party. I cooked and things seemed to be moving in the right direction. All of Levi's cousins were super excited for him and so far, they liked me. Especially his girl cousins, they said finally he's gotten over his ex and he can give them a baby cousin. I didn't want kids so I just changed the subject.

Well they all spoke too soon I found out a little while later that I was pregnant. Levi told his mom and brothers and they were excited for us. I didn't really know how to feel because having kids wasn't part of my plan but the baby was coming so I had to figure it out. Out the blue Momma Nikki called me and said she had a letter for me to read. I told her to come to my job because I wasn't even supposed to be talking to her. I didn't want to make Levi mad so I didn't tell him.

Honestly, I was a little surprised to hear from Momma Nikki I hadn't talked to her in a while. My first love wrote me saying he was still in love with me and he missed me. I was so excited but I was in a whole new relationship and I was pregnant so what was I supposed to do? This is what I didn't want to happen for him to come to his senses and I had already made another commitment. I left the letter with Momma Nikki and we caught up a little but I didn't tell her I was pregnant. She told me he was going to be getting out soon.

CHAPTER 8

A few weeks had passed and Levi called me to pick him up from his mom's house. He said that he needed to talk to me. I could tell by his voice it wasn't good news. When I got to his mom's house no one could find him. I walked outside and Allison came flying through the gate. She started cussing me out and calling me a bitch. I socked her in her mouth. I surprised myself I had never been in a fight in my life.

LEVI'S BROTHERS RAN OUTSIDE AND BROKE IT APART SAYING YOU can't fight her. She's a kid and she's pregnant. Levi came out of nowhere and yelled at his brother for grabbing me. That's when he told me Allison was pregnant and it was his baby. I was so heart broken. He lied to me and I was stupid enough to believe him. I hopped in my car and left. I went to the liquor store on my way home. I bought a cigar and a pint of Hennessey.

I WAS CRYING HYSTERICALLY AND I COULDN'T THINK STRAIGHT. I went home and started packing my stuff. I started drinking

Hennessy and just crying and crying. Levi's brother Joshua walked in the door and snatched it from me and told me I was tripping and I needed to calm down. That I was pregnant and he didn't want anything to happen to his niece or nephew. He handed me his blunt and told me to hit it so I did. That was the first time I ever smoked weed in my life.

THEIR COUSIN WAS THROWING A PARTY AND HIS OTHER COUSIN came and picked me and Joshua up from the house. While we were at the party Levi apologized for lying to me and he told me that she was just going to be his baby-mama. That he wanted to be with me and not her. I didn't feel right. I was cramping badly. Of course, I believed him and I forgave him.

A FEW DAYS LATER I WENT TO THE DOCTOR AND I WAS HAVING A miscarriage I had to have a DNC done. I was so sad. When I got home, Levi hugged and kissed me and he said when the time was right we would have our baby. There was an unexpected knock on the door. He opened it and it was Allison I was pissed. Why was she at my door? How did she know where I lived? She had this smirk look on her face. I slammed the door in her face and blocked Levi from going outside.

LEVI WAS MAD AND TOLD ME I WASN'T ABOUT TO KEEP HIM FROM his child. I was pissed because I just lost my baby and here this bitch was at my door and I'm supposed to be okay with it. He went outside and came back in after thirty minutes. His nephew was having a birthday party at Chuck-e-Cheese. I didn't really want to go because I knew that Allison was going to be there, she knew his immediate family a lot longer than I did.

. . .

FRANCES DUPREE

When it was time to leave, Levi road with Allison's ride and told me to meet him at his moms to pick him up so we could go home. That he just wanted to make sure she went straight home. This made me so mad. Everyone knew that I had just lost my baby but no one showed any sign of sympathy and it seemed as though Levi was just rubbing him and Allison's baby in my face. So many times, I contemplated leaving and starting all over somewhere that no one knew me. Levi and I didn't have any ties our baby died. But the thought of being alone was scarier and more hurtful then what I was dealing with.

CHAPTER 9

When Levi and I would have sex, he would always say he wanted me to have his baby. I told him I wanted my baby back and I would start to cry while we were having sex and he would tell me to stop because he hated to hear me cry. I bought ovulation tests so I would know when I could get pregnant. He didn't know this though. I was sitting at home alone one day and my phone rang. It was my first love; I was so excited and I had to see him. Levi was gone at his mom's house so he would never know.

I LEFT TO GO MEET UP WITH MY FIRST LOVE. AS SOON AS I SAW him, I hugged and kissed him and told him how much I missed him. I also told him about Levi which he already knew and wasn't happy about because he knew he wasn't really treating me right and he was cheating. We made love as if we never missed a beat. He still knew how to sling that dick, how to touch me in all the right ways, kiss me as if I was his one and only, and later I reluctantly had to go home. I went home and showered and Levi never knew I was gone. I had dinner on the table ready when he walked in.

He was pissed and drunk when he came home. Come to find out he was at his moms waiting on Allison all day and she never showed up. He thought something had happened to her. She finally got home and called him and said she had gone to the hospital to get checked out that she wasn't feeling well. He told her he was going to stay the night with his mom. I was pissed and we started arguing and I tried to stop him. That was a big mistake. He grabbed me by my hair and threw me into our glass closet door and it broke. I was in shock. I never thought he was that type of guy. This was the first time he had ever put his hands on me and I would soon find out it wouldn't be the last. From this moment forward I no longer looked at him as my knight in shining armor.

He left and I fell to the floor crying. I didn't hear from him for two days. When he finally contacted me he apologized and said he was stupid and he was drunk and he would never put his hands on me again. I called my first love and he picked me up, after riding around with him for a while we ended our time together in the back seat of his car. It was kind of exciting because Levi was on the next street over on nineteen street and we were on sunrise. Again, I went home as if nothing had happened.

CHAPTER 10

My period didn't come and I was pregnant, but I was being ratchet and hooking up with my first love and then going home to Levi. I thought it was my first loves but I wasn't sure because I had slept with Levi more. Even though my heart and soul felt one way my mind tried to convince me of another way. My first love would pick me up and take me to Fontana to my doctor's appointments. We would hang out for a while but eventually I had to go home.

LEVI BEGGED ME TO GET AN ABORTION HE SAID HE ALREADY HAD A baby coming and he was going to be with me but two babies around the same time was too much, that he would look bad and I told him no. That if I had to, I would raise my baby on my own. He got mad and left to his mom's house. I started to have a panic attack and the overwhelming feeling of not being good enough for anyone to truly love me came back. I was crying hysterically and could hardly breathe. I went in the kitchen and grabbed the sharpest knife I could find and I cut my arm up. It was such a relief from the pain that I was feeling. I heard a voice in my head say, "I will never leave you nor for sake you." I finally calmed down. I cleaned and bandage my arm and went to Levi's mom's house.

LEVI GOT MAD AND TOLD ME TO GO HOME AND I TOLD HIM NO. He pulled me by my shirt to the car and when we got in the car port I refused to leave. He started to choke me and I fell he started kicking me in my legs. One of his brothers saw and they came and snatched him up and told me to leave. I drove home crying the whole way there. I told myself I was done with him because he kept putting his hands on me. But when he apologized, I took him back

HE CAME HOME ONE DAY ON A RAMPAGE HIS BROTHERS BEST friend Hannah told him that she saw me at Kaiser with my first love and that it wasn't his baby. I told him she was lying that I went to the doctor by myself. She was so mad and wanted to fight me but he wouldn't let her because I was pregnant. I had to figure out what to do. My first love was not going anywhere because it could be his baby and I wanted to be with Levi I had built a life with him. I had to make a choice and do it quick.

THE NEXT TIME MY FIRST LOVE CALLED AS MUCH AS IT TORE ME up, I lied and said I had a miscarriage. He breathed in real hard and simply hung up the phone. I spent the next few months trying to convince Levi that it was his baby and to keep him home with me because every other day he was at his moms with Allison. For some dumb reason I thought the fact that I was having this baby would make Levi and I closer, but it seemed as though we were further apart than ever. His main focus was on

Allison and their baby and when he had the time on me and ours.

IN MY HEART AND SOUL I KNEW THAT MY BABY BELONGED TO MY first love but my mind didn't want to believe it. My first love had his own life and I wasn't sure if he was in a relationship as I did mine and it was time to face facts and I had to try and keep my relationship together. I felt guilty but at the time I felt as though I was making the right choice for all parties involved. Later I would learn that was the worst move that I could have made and my son would suffer because of it.

I LEFT TO HANG OUT WITH MY OLD FRIEND ALLAH AND I WAS gone all day. I had a really good time catching up with her and enjoyed the conversation. Most of all it was a break from my life and I really needed it. When I got home Levis' brothers were acting weird and my room door was locked. Levi was in there but his brothers wouldn't let me go near my door. Then out of nowhere one of them said they left something in my car. We walked to my car and came back and the door was open and Levi had this disgusting smirk look on his face. We started arguing and he and his brothers all left for his mom's house in lil Africa.

CHAPTER 11

Through my pregnancy the road wasn't easy at all. I ended up losing my apartment because I didn't pay the rent. I had lost my job because I stopped going to work like I was supposed to because I was too busy watching Levi. We ended up moving in with Levi's brother Jaxon and his girlfriend Violet. Staying there wasn't easy and it was very embarrassing as well. Especially because the night that we moved Levi and I got into a fist fight. Levi took my car after the fight and left on my way to Violet's house. I tried to jump in front of several cars but none of them hit me. I was so overwhelmed with emotion and I was so tired of being hurt but I wouldn't leave him because I was afraid to be alone.

I felt so dumb the next morning waking up there and Levi wasn't with me he was with Allison. Violet's best friend Apple had a brother and I thought he was so cute we flirted but nothing ever happened because I was pregnant and I didn't want to cheat. I was really trying to make my relationship work. I told Apple that I wanted to fuck her brother but I told her it was a fantasy that would never happen.

Levi came back the next day and he sat on the couch and I was ignoring him. At the time I had nowhere else to go. My dad wasn't really talking to me. When I found out I was having a boy I automatically was going to name him after Levi, so I got Levi's name tattooed on my back. My dad saw it and was pissed. He went off and told me to get out of his house. For the life of me I couldn't understand why my dad was so mad at me. Momma Nikki always had her door open to me but it didn't feel right. So, I just sucked it up and took it. Levi texted my phone and said he was sorry. I was like putty in his hands and again I forgave him.

My birthday came and Levi and I were supposed to go out. Allison knew it was my birthday and all of a sudden, she wanted Levi to watch their daughter. I was pissed, she knew it was my birthday and I know she did it on purpose. When we got back to Levi's brother's house we got into a huge argument and he told me he knew for sure that was his daughter but he didn't know if my son was his. Talking out the side of my neck I told him that wasn't his daughter and I hoped I was there the day he found out, not knowing this day would actually come to pass.

I finally found another apartment "The Rain Trees" but because I had an eviction on my name, I needed a co-signer. There was no one I could call but Levi. He was saying he wasn't sure if he wanted to continue to be with me. I immediately started crying and I told him that he owed me that I moved him out of his mom's house. I told him that he was sad and pathetic because he would allow me and his son to be homeless. He said no I'll sign for you but don't expect me to live there and I said well see about that. Even though that was both of our apartment he didn't spend a lot of time there unless he was throwing a party.

Levi, Violet and I went to the mall and I was dressed super cute. I wanted to take pregnancy pictures but Levi wasn't having it. We walked around the whole mall. He dropped me off at home and he gave Violet a ride to work and he went to work. I started having contractions so I called Levi but he refused to leave work. I called my dad but he was out of the state. I called the ambulance and they had to kick the door in to get to me. I was really in labor and I was scared to be by myself.

I refused all the medicine except for what went into the IV. As soon as I pushed him out Levi walked in the room. They handed my son to him and I went off just because he's black doesn't mean he's the dad. Don't just hand my son to anyone. Levi looked at him and said, "This isn't my son. His ears are so big. He is white and he has smoky grey eyes". I said, "Yes he is." Levi didn't believe me.

Levi wouldn't stay with us in the hospital he left but when he came back that night, he came with his brother Jaxon and bought me pizza. I was in the hospital for three days. Levi's immediate family all came to the hospital to see the baby, but overall it was just me and my son. The time came to pick his name and I was going to name him after Levi and he told me no. He said don't even give that baby my last name.

He came to the hospital and he was drunk. He looked at my son and said this isn't my son he looks like a grey rat and he has big ass ears. My ears are small. He asked, "Are you sure this is my son?" and I said, "Yes"! He held our son close and began to cry, he said that he wanted his first born to be a boy. That he didn't want a girl because he knew eventually, he would have to kill a nigga behind her. To my surprise he stayed with us until visiting hours were over, the nurse told him that since he was the father that he could stay the night but he refused and said he would be back first thing in the morning.

On the birth record I originally named our son Levi Orion Lockwood Jr. But when Levi came to the hospital, he told me not to name my son after him because he wasn't sure if he was his. I immediately started crying and I said after everything you put me through when I was pregnant, you weren't there when I gave birth to our son, and now you want to come up here and pull this bullshit. Our son could have died from all the times you put your hands on me. He said name him Tristan because he's a miracle after everything I put you through while you were pregnant, he kissed me on my forehead and said I apologize.

CHAPTER 12

The first few days and nights at home were rough. I wasn't prepared for the late-night feedings and diaper changes. But to my surprise Levi was great with our son at night when he was home with us. He knew that I was an early bird so he would stay up drinking patron and hypnotic, watch cartoons and stay up with our son. My boobs were so hard and swollen and they hurt so bad, I got so scared and I thought they were going to explode.

Levi wouldn't let me take my son to his mom's house. First he said that he was to young and he didn't want him out and getting sick, then he said that to many noisy people are at his moms and he didn't want them to know what our son looked like, then he lied and told me that his mom didn't want my son over there because she didn't think he was her grandson. One day his mom called me and asked me why I didn't want my baby at her house? I was so confused and told her that wasn't true. That Levi told me she didn't want my son at her house because she wasn't sure if he was her grandson. She said that he was lying and she was going to beat his ass.

I told her that I was having a hard time, that when Levi was around, he was a big help but when he wasn't it was hard for me. I started to cry. I told her that I thought my boobs were going to explode because they were so hard and that they hurt so much. She told me to put hot towels on them so the milk would drain, and to eat toast and that would help as well. I told her every time my son would suck on my boobs all I would do is cry because it hurt so bad. She said give him a bottle and I said no breastfeeding is healthier. She said she was going to come stay with me for a few days.

Levi's mom came to stay with us for a few days and she put hot towels on my breast to get the milk to come down. She cooked, cleaned, and took over with the baby. I told her that I was so grateful because I didn't have my mom to come stay with me and help me. At that moment I felt like our relationship went to a whole new level, it felt as though I was her daughter. For a short period, things were good at home Levi went to work and would come home. He would stay up with the baby at night. I thought for a moment we were finally on good terms and were going to be a family but that was short lived.

A few weeks passed and Levi's phone was blowing up. It was Allison saying she was on her way. I made it clear to everyone I didn't want her to know where my apartment was. I didn't want him to leave. The doctor's said not to have sex for six weeks but I felt I had to do something to get him to stay so he and I had sex on the couch while Alison was banging on the door. He ended up leaving with her anyway. They caught the bus to the west side of San Bernardino so she could buy him shoes. I was mad because our son had a doctor's appointment and of course Levi didn't show up. Our son had RSV and had to be hospitalized. I was blowing Levi up but he wasn't answering. When he finally called, I told him and he came to the hospital but he had Allison with him.

I went off, "Why the fuck would you bring her up here? Whatever is going on with our son isn't her business." I told her not to come into the room. She ended up walking back home by herself and he stayed for a couple hours. Our son was in there for a week. He would come to visit at least once a day for a few hours but he would never stay the night. My nana popped up one day I didn't even know she was coming. I told her I was going home to shower. I had been calling Levi all night, morning and afternoon and he didn't answer. My nana said she would stay for an hour then she was leaving for me to hurry up.

I walked in my house and Allison Levi and his cousin was sitting on my couch and I went off. I told Allison to get the fuck out of my house and as she was walking away, she started talking big shit. I was following behind her. I grabbed her by her ponytail and slung her on the floor and started punching her in the face and hitting her head on the ground. Her eyes started rolling in the back of her head I freaked out and started crying, I was yelling for someone to call the ambulance.

I was so scared I just knew I was going to go to jail. I rushed back to the hospital by this time my nana was gone. Through the grace of God, the police never came for me. But a nasty rumor started that my aunt and I jumped Allison but my aunt and I weren't even talking at the time. She never even knew my son was in the hospital. I guess it was that hard for everyone to believe I beat her up on my own. Later I found out she had a concussion and a blood vessel in her eye pooped. When she first woke up she didn't even know who her daughter was.

It was months later before Levi told me that he was upset about the fight between Allison and I. We were arguing one day and out of the blue he said my baby mama and her sitters are going to jump you just like you and your aunt jumped her. They wanted to kill you. You're lucky that she lived. I said they have seen me several times since this has happened and none of them have said anything to me about it. I said if you were feeling some type of way you should have been said something this is like four months old. Levi grabbed my car keys and took off.

MARRYING OUTSIDE OF GOD'S WILL

I cleaned up the house but I was still so angry, how dare he disrespect me and just take off in my car. I was over the bullshit; I was blowing up his phone and I kept telling him that I wanted my car and I knew he was at his moms and Tristan and I were gonna walk over there to get my car. I started walking from Sterling and Baseline toward Highland and Nineteen Street. On our way there we passed a little small bridge kind of it was rocks and water running over it. I stood there for a little while and I kept thinking the world would be better off without my son and I in it. That my son didn't deserve the life I had brought him into, no one loved him or me. I saw myself jump to our death holding him and all I heard in my head is "I will never leave you nor forsake you" I cried like a baby and turned around with my baby and walked back home.

CHAPTER 13

Several months had passed since I had Tristan at this point, he was walking around in his walker and I hadn't had a period yet. I called the doctor and asked if it was normal and he said yes that when you are breastfeeding it will throw your period off. A couple weeks had gone by and I was at work and I got really dizzy and I was on the verge of passing out. I called Levi and he came to pick me up. Levi took me to the doctor and they said that I was pregnant. I was so hurt and I was mad, I really didn't want any additional kids.

I DIDN'T KNOW WHAT TO THINK BECAUSE IT WAS HARD FOR ME TO take care of the son that I already had. Between the ups and downs with Levi, trying to work and I was contemplating going back to school, then when I had our son by myself I kept thinking I didn't grow up with my mom, and really had no idea what I was doing. I always prayed and asked God to not let me destroy my son's life. With all this going on, how was I going to take care of another child? I didn't even like kids and now I was going to have two babies. Levi told me to get an abortion and I

MARRYING OUTSIDE OF GOD'S WILL

told him no that it was a sin and I wasn't going to get an abortion. I kept saying that I hope this is my baby girl. The whole time I was pregnant, I was miserable because I didn't want the baby but since I was keeping the baby I prayed this one was a girl.

I WAS NINE MONTHS PREGNANT WITH MY SECOND SON AND I HAD a warrant. For the most part I was a good teenager and didn't get into trouble. But when I became an adult, I started to do all of my dirt. I got caught stealing out of Macy's and I went to court and was on probation but I didn't follow their terms of the probation and this resulted in a warrant. I went to court and they took me to jail. They said that I violated probation because I didn't check in and I had caught a new case. While in West Valley Detention center I went into labor. I crawled up on the floor crying, my cellmate presses the button and told the guards she thought I was in labor. They took me to arrowhead and I had Mason. I stayed in the hospital with him for three days but I had to go back to jail and I had to call someone to come and get my son.

THAT WAS THE HARDEST THING I HAD TO DO, I FELT LIKE THAT was my karma because I didn't want my son and the whole time I was pregnant I didn't bond with him or anything. I named him Mason Angel Lockwood I called my pastors wife and she came and got my son. While I was pregnant, I didn't want him but when I was holding him in my arms all of that went away. I just wanted to love him and hold him and give him the world. He was my angel because despite all the bad he still was a perfect gift from God.

. . .

FRANCES DUPREE

I went back to my cell and I cried and prayed and cried. I asked God to forgive me for not wanting my son. That just because I felt a certain way about Levi, I shouldn't have felt that way about my son. It was so hard not being able to be with Mason. I didn't know what was going to happen when I went to court and I wanted the opportunity to build a relationship with him.

My birthday came and I was surprised I had a visitor. It was my dad. I didn't even know that my dad knew where I was. We talked for a little while I apologized to him for all the wrong, I had done and he put $100 on my books. My dad didn't know at the time that I just had another baby. I didn't tell him because I knew he would be mad and I didn't want him to cut me off again.

When I went to court, I went home. Levi picked me up and I hugged Tristian and cried and my first destination was getting my baby Mason. We went to the pastor's house and when I got there, his wife gave me my son and I was filled with so much joy. God had answered my prayers and I would be able to build a relationship with my baby. I was so overjoyed. I promised my sons that I would be a better mom to both of them.

CHAPTER 14

We ended up getting evicted from the Raintree apartments because they said that there was too much traffic coming in and out of my apartment. I had to figure out where I and my two children were going to stay. Levis mom said that we could stay with her, Levi and I ended up putting everything from our apartment in storage. His mom told me that I needed to go and apply for the county again. The first time that I applied they denied me and said that I was lying about my situation.

I went back and this time I asked to speak with a supervisor. I told them that I had been evicted and she asked me for the paperwork and I gave it to her. She called my old job and they told her that I wasn't working anymore because I just had my second child, but they did expect me back to work soon. Levi and I had gotten into an argument right before I went to the county because I was asking for his help to find another place for his kids to live, but instead he'd rather go shopping with Allison.

God is always an on-time God. Not only did the supervisor approve my case, but she back paid me from the time I applied until current for the cash aid and the food stamps. By the time I left the county I had $5,000 in cash and $1,200 in food stamps. I drove close to Redlands and the boys and I got a room. We stayed in the room until we found an apartment in Moreno Valley. After a week of not hearing from Levi, he finally called me one night he was drunk and he said that he was being shot at and I needed to come and get him right away. I could hear the gun shots in the background. I went off on him, I told him that he didn't care where my boys and I were living and I didn't care what he had going on and I hung up in his face.

The boys and I moved to Moreno Valley and it were about a month before I allowed Levi to come. Of course, this was a problem because Allison swore that I purposely moved him away from his daughters, but the only reason that I wanted him to come was so he could watch the kids while I went to work. I had got another job in Riverside. The first night he got there he was pissy drunk and he grabbed one of the kitchen knives and he held it to my throat. He told me to pray to my God because that is where he was going to send me. I was scared straight on the inside but I was so angry because I had to practically beg him to watch his kids so I could go to work. I told him to do whatever he felt that he needed to do.

He wanted to have sex that night and I didn't want to and this made him really mad. He started to cuss me out and call me all kinds of hoes and bitches telling me that he could have any bitch that he wanted, and that I was lucky that he wasted his time on me. He got mad and hopped in my car and left. I had to call off of work and I ended up losing my job because he stayed gone in my car for three days. I was blowing up his phone to come back because my WIC folder was in the car and my baby needed milk. He didn't come so I ended up having to borrow money from someone in order to buy my son a can of milk. He finally came back later. I found out because he and Allison had gotten into it and my stupid self-took him back.

MARRYING OUTSIDE OF GOD'S WILL

We would often go visit Levis mom, moving to Moreno Valley didn't seem like a good idea anymore because now that I had taken Levi back when I wasn't working, we were always at his mom's house in San Bernardino. One night I was tired and ready to go and he still wanted to hang out. I put our two sons in their car seats and I was just going to leave him there. Since he wanted to be on the block so bad, he could stay and I would take our boys home. Well this turned out to be a very bad idea because as soon as I was about to drive off Levi came out of nowhere and kicked in my driver side window. All of the glass flew in the back seat on the boys.

I was freaking out; I was scared it would get in their eyes and they would get cut. Levis uncle was pissed, he picked him up by his throat and slammed him on the concrete. His mom helped me clean the glass off the kids and out of their car seats. I wasn't able to go home because of the broken window. I drove to a friend's house and she let me and the boys stay the night. The next morning Levi called me and apologized and said that he had a hangover. That he wanted me to take him to pick up his check so he could pay to get my window fixed.

I ended up moving back to San Bernardino into some apartments on Pumalo. I was pregnant with my third child. I was so upset because I was on birth control. It would be just my luck that birth control would fail me and I was pregnant for the third time. When I moved in it was mainly just me and the kids. Levi rarely came over him and I had an explosive argument over the phone, I called him and told him that I was putting Tristan in Preschool so for now on he couldn't just see my kids whenever he wanted that the boys were going to be on a schedule. He went off and he told me that I didn't have the right to tell him when he could and when he couldn't see his kids.

After hanging up with him I didn't want to bring another kid into this world arguing and going back and forth with this man. He was making it more than clear through his actions that my children and I were a convenience to him. I started calling different adoption agencies and setting up interviews. My mind set was if I can find my third child a good loving family then my third child wouldn't have to go through the back and forth and pain that my other children were going through. I scheduled the interviews and was fully prepared mentally and emotionally to give my son up for adoption.

I went on the adoption interviews and the agencies gave me donated clothes and toys for my other boys and gas cards. They kept up with me to check on me after every doctor's appointment and before I would leave the office, they would pray over me and my children. We hadn't found a family for my son yet but they assured me that by the time I had him we would have found the perfect family for him.

One day when I picked Tristan up from preschool, I stopped in the Parcilla's Helping Hands office and signed up for their case management program. I also enrolled in online school with the University of Phoenix. I told my case worker that I was in the process of putting my third son up for adoption, she asked me how his father felt about it and I told her that he didn't care. She said that her prayer was that God would change my heart.

There was a computer lab there so I would drop off Tristan and head straight to the computer to do my work while he was in school and we would go home when he was out. This was our routine for a while and it was great. I started attending Ecclesia Christian Fellowship. I started praying more, going to church, and focusing on me and the kids. Life seemed to be leveling it's self out and the kids and I were doing great.

Levi finally called and I was hesitant to answer the phone at first but I knew the kids missed their dad. It seemed like as soon as I was finally getting back on my feet and life was headed in the right direction here he comes. I answered and he asked if he could see the kids. I gave him a real hard time at first but eventually I agreed to let him come to the house so that he could see the kids. He woke up in the morning and took Tristan to school and then he kept Mason while I did my work. When he acted like this it made me miss us. We were having sex one night and he had to call the ambulance because I went into labor.

He came to the hospital and he was so in love with our son, when I held him, I started crying and I told him that I couldn't give my baby up for adoption and he said good because he wasn't going to sign the paper anyway. I laughed and said I didn't need you to sign anything you're not my husband and you're so quick to deny my kids it was a choice that I was making on my own. Leo was the light of our lives and Levi said he wanted to stay home and we were going to be a family.

CHAPTER 15

I moved off of Pumalo into some apartments called the Trap this time it wasn't because of me being irresponsible but because paperwork wasn't turned in on time and I didn't have the money in time to pay the rent. They were called this because there was one way in and one way out. When Levi came to see where I had moved, he said the apartments were raggedy and he would be dammed if he was going to live like that. I was pissed because he didn't help me find a new place and he wasn't giving me money to pay for rent or bills or to take care of our sons so why would he be judgmental.

I became good friends with the neighbor and she would help me from time to time with the boys. The drama continued between Levi and me. He would mainly come over when he and Allison got into it. At this time, we were together but we weren't. But anytime he needed me I was there. One night him and Allison got into a fight and I walked over to his moms in the middle of the night to go and get him pregnant and all. His cousin said dame your pregnant again I said yeah, he said you just love having babies I said no I don't believe in abortion and I was on the pill took it as directed and still

MARRYING OUTSIDE OF GOD'S WILL

ended up pregnant. He laughed and said that's all bad. But we know it's a boy so it's cool we got another shoulder on our team.

Allison tried to run up on me and fight me and his brother came grabbed her threw her over his shoulder and took her back to the house. My neighbor sat with my kids while I went on this mission. The whole thing was stupid and a waste of time because their daughter had a doctor appointment the next morning and he went right back over there.

Levi didn't like the neighbors and he said they were noisy and messy. I really think he didn't like the fact that she used to tell me not to put up with his bullshit. She used to always tell me that just because I had three kids and one on the way didn't mean that someone else wouldn't want me. That I shouldn't sit around waiting on my baby daddy and obviously he only came around when he wanted something that's not love.

My neighbor's brother Porter started coming around and he was fine. We use to flirt back and forth but when Levi would come around, we would argue and fight a lot and Porter didn't like how Levi talked and treated me. Levis favorite word to call me was Bitch. That was my name to him instead of calling me babe or anything else when he was angry.

A few days before Valentine's Day I took the kids to Levi's mom's house and I left with his brother's baby mama Hillary. We went shopping at target. I was telling her that my neighbor was going to throw a Valentine's Day party and that she should go with me. Next thing you know I get a call from Levis mom saying that he got arrested and we needed to hurry up and get to her house and get our kids.

Levis mom was pissed the police were there looking for her brother and they ran everybody's name in the house. Levi had an old warrant because when we got into a fight and he hit me I called the police. I felt so bad that he was in jail this fight happened five years ago and I had completely forgotten about it.

I made sure he had money on his books. I bought prepaid credit cards so he was able to call me and I wrote him every day.

At the time we weren't on the best of terms or even together but I still loved him and didn't want to see him in jail. I went to my neighbor's valentine's party and she had a stripper come. We had so much fun. For once I was being a young adult and having fun not worrying about where Levi was, what he was doing or stressing behind the kids. My neighbor's brother Porter came by that night and it happened, I sat on his lap and we started kissing. I pulled off his shirt and he pulled off my clothes. We both agreed to keep it between him and me.

He knew about Levi and I knew about his baby-mama that he was with but they broke up over something stupid. We were both attracted to each other for a while. We were always flirting with each other but it seemed like every time we were around each other Levi would pop up out of nowhere. Levi was in jail at the moment and we weren't really together anyways so I was doing me. He flipped me over on the bed licked me a few times and was giving it to me. But then he stopped he said it wasn't right and we shouldn't be doing this because he knew I was going to get back with Levi and he was going to get back with his baby mamma.

After that when I would see him, I would just go in my apartment and I wouldn't speak to him. He walked up on me one time at the dumpster while I was taking my trash out. He didn't understand why I was ignoring him and he said that he liked me and if I wanted to give it a try, he would be with me but he didn't want to get caught up between Levi and I. He said he could see himself with me but he knew I wasn't going to leave Levi alone and that was going to be a problem. He didn't want to have to hurt him and he already wanted to fight him because of how disrespectful he was to me and that I was a good woman.

Levi's court date came and I caught the bus to the court

house. I tried talking to his public defender but he wouldn't talk to me because I was the victim in the case so I had to speak with the district attorney. I told her that I wanted the charges dropped. That this incident happened over five years ago and that we had reconciled since and I wouldn't cooperate with them. She said okay and he was out that night. He came home and I told him about the valentine's party and he was pissed because he said he was sitting in jail and I was out partying. We started arguing and he was about to leave but I walked outside behind him arguing and being loud.

His phone rang and it was Allison. She was talking so loud through the phone that I heard the whole conversation. She told him that she didn't need him and the baby she was pregnant with she would raise with or without him. I really went off because I didn't know she was pregnant and he tried to say that I was listening so hard that I was hearing stuff.

My neighbor came out and she said that her baby daddy was in the house trying to keep her brother from coming out and if he did end up coming out, I better not get in the middle of it or her and I was going to have a problem. I told her at the end of the day Levi was the father of my kids and I wasn't going to let nobody put their hands on him. So, if we were going to have a problem it is what it is and I was going to ride with him until the end. She and I didn't talk after that day. I moved out a few months later.

For the next couple of years Levi would continue to go back and forth between Allison and I. We would have children in the same year. She ended up with three girls and I had six sons. My first love and I would have a few run-ins but no more of us sleeping together. He would just pop up out of nowhere. Every time I couldn't help but blush because I was still in love with him. I would tease him and say he was stalking me but I was always happy to see him. He made it a point to let me know if I or the kids ever needed anything and he had us.

I wasn't stable and I kept moving every few months. I would do well by paying my rent on time figuring the bills out and making sure my kids had what they needed. But after a while I would go back to being irresponsible and not pay the full rent. I'd pay a little here and there and I kept getting evicted as a result. Sometimes I wish that I was taught all of these things about being a mother and an adult, and why I was so damned hard headed and didn't get the point. Rent gets paid before anything. Honestly, I think I was that way because after leaving my mom house I moved every year.

I always dealt with things head on. I had a restraining order on her because I was tired of always being the one dealing with consequences but not always being the one causing problems and my children had suffered enough but today, I just didn't care. I wanted the truth. I was tired of the games and all of the back and forth. The good no longer outweighed the bad. How did the tables end up turning? For the first time in this stupid triangle I was chasing Levi and he was chasing Rena. Usually Levi is chasing me and Allison is chasing him. We were at their daughter's school when I pulled up and I was pissed.

He looked me in my face and he said, "Allison is my girl", words I thought I would never hear him say. I took off on him and I was fighting him in the parking lot. Of course, after all these years this was funny to Allison. She called the police because of the restraining order but God. They allowed Levi to call someone so my two cars weren't towed. I was left walking home and Allison and her sisters drove past me and were laughing.

That's when God told me it was time to leave San Bernardino because if I didn't either I would end up killing her or she would end up killing me because the back and forth wouldn't end. One thing I don't do is play with God. I started packing up my house. I didn't know where I was moving quite yet. I just knew I had to get out of there.

MARRYING OUTSIDE OF GOD'S WILL

I saw on Facebook that my kids' cousin's mom had moved up the hill to Adelanto so I inboxed her and asked her how she liked it? How the schools were and how the cost of living was. She gave me great reviews, so that's where I was going to move. I immediately started looking for houses in Adelanto. At the time I was working for Colonial Life as an Administrative Assistant. God was so good to me because I was on an ankle monitor because I kept not reporting to probation, so since I had kids and was technically a single mom, I was on house arrest instead of going to jail. I had also enrolled in online classes to obtain my AA in paralegal studies. Through it all I never lost my dream of becoming an attorney. I knew being a paralegal would get my foot in the door.

I found many beautiful houses for a good price but one stuck out to me in particular. A three-bedroom two bath for eight hundred. I knew this was nothing but God because there was such a smooth transition. I called and told the property management I was moving from San Bernardino I worked full-time and could I do everything by fax. They agreed I faxed all my income they asked for current landlord information. I gave a friend's number and she gave me such an excellent reference that they didn't even run my credit.

Levi saw I wasn't playing and I was really about to move. I told him he could come with or stay I didn't care but this was a move I had to make. I also told him if he was to move with me, we needed to get married. That this was going to be a fresh start and I wasn't making that move taking the same drama with me. At this point him and Allison were at odds and even though he didn't want to move to the high desert he didn't want to be stuck down there and have to live with his mom either.

Levi didn't know this whole time Allison was writing and taking calls from her first love while he was in prison. So, when he got out he went to be with her. Allison told Levi that she wanted him and her first love. He told her that she had to choose so she packed all Levi stuff that was at her house and had it waiting for him at the door. I gave her respect because the whole time he thought he was playing us but she was playing him. This made him go from wanting us both to wanting mainly her but the funny part was she wanted both of them.

CHAPTER 16

In Levis eyes I was a saint so he tried to really make us work. He started talking to his step brother who was in the NFL so we drove to Arizona to one of his games. We had a really good time lots of love and laughs. His brother left tickets for us at the box office and we sat in the family section with his wife and their friends. Meeting his wife was such a wonderful experience she welcomed us with so much love and made sure we were comfortable. I instantly took to her. After the game we went to eat and I met his brother for the first time and we had so much fun. We had to come right back because I had to work the next morning but we promised to return to visit.

BY THIS TIME MY DAD HAD FINALLY ACCEPTED LEVI AND WE HAD decided to get married but I told Levi he had to get my dad's permission or we couldn't. A small part of me was hoping my dad said no because in my heart I knew God didn't want me to marry Levi. I also knew that if I married Levi I would be out of God's will because I was acting out of disobedience. I even reached out to my first love's mom to see what was up with him because if he actually wanted to give us a try I wouldn't marry Levi. She told me to go ahead and get married that he was a rolling stone like his dad. That she loved his dad the way that I loved him.

IN MY HEART AND MIND ONCE I SAID I DO THAT WAS IT. MY DAD said yes and I got nowhere with my first love and so Levi and I were getting married. My aunt and my nana took me to hang out to get my nails done, my hair was already done and to buy a dress. Levi was pissed because we had gone and bought a dress but I didn't really like it. I reached out to Levi's cousin and asked him to put something together for Levi and he wasn't going to be able to make the wedding.

WHEN WE GOT MARRIED MY SISTER, DAD, NANA, AUNT, FRIEND, all six of our sons, Levis lil sister and lil brother came to the wedding. We went to Levi's mom's house to get her and she didn't come. No one else in his family came and he was really hurt. After the wedding we went to Applebees to eat and that is when most of his family came. Levi was still pissed and of course he was taking a lot of mess.

THE NEXT DAY WAS LEVI'S LITTLE COUSIN'S BIRTHDAY AND HIS cousin was throwing a huge party. We didn't go because his cousin stayed right across the way from Allison. But the majority of Levis' family went. We went to his mom's house and they argued. He told her how he was hurt no one showed up at our wedding but everyone was going to a one-year old's birthday party. His mom said she didn't care and she was going to go.

MARRYING OUTSIDE OF GOD'S WILL

. . .

LEVI AND I GOT INTO A STUPID ARGUMENT I DON'T EVEN remember why to be honest but I ended up spending the night at my job and he left the house. At the time I didn't know where he went but I would later find out he spent the night with Allison. The day had come for me to go to Adelanto to look at the house and if I liked it to pay my deposit. Levi knew what I was doing and told me to pick him up from his moms. I told him that we needed to get an annulment we both knew this marriage wasn't going to work and we shouldn't waste anymore of each other's time. He could see his kids on the weekends. Just let me and the kids move and live a peaceful and happy life. Levi convinced me to pick him up.

WE WEREN'T ON THE BEST TERMS BUT HE WAS STILL MY HUSBAND at the end of the day so I listened. I loved the house but he didn't because it wasn't San Bernardino. In any case; I paid my deposit because I was moving with or without him. His little brother was living with us which he had been for many years and his girlfriend. When it was time to move, they both moved with us.

CHAPTER 17

I found out I was pregnant but I already had six kids and didn't want any more so I went and had an abortion while I was at work. I went to the clinic and took the first pill there and the second one at work and not too long after all that I felt a splash and that was it, the baby was gone. This probably sounds heartless but I didn't feel bad at all. I was actually relieved. I just couldn't understand how birth control could keep failing me. I didn't want any more kids; my six sons were enough.

To me in my heart six kids was enough to say the least. They were too much sometimes but I loved my boys and wouldn't have it any other way. I always wanted a daughter but at this point I didn't think it was going to happen. My mother-in-law would tell me God wasn't going to give me a daughter because I didn't accept Levi's daughters. That was a very touchy subject for me because he cheated on me to make the last two.

We officially made the move from San Bernardino to Adelanto. I, however; still worked down the hill. I had the kids enrolled in school already and I signed them up for baseball so

MARRYING OUTSIDE OF GOD'S WILL

while we were moving, they were at tryouts. That's how smooth the transition was so I knew it was nothing but God. Levi hadn't seen his daughters in a while and trying to be a good wife I reached out to Allison. That wasn't a good idea at all and I didn't fully prepare myself for the way she was going to respond.

It didn't go so well, she told me how she knew where I worked. She used to meet Levi all the time in front of my job. That the night we got into a fight right after we got married, that they slept together and she was pregnant. But I didn't get angry. I just let her know I was his wife and she needed to know her place and to stay in her lane. That if this was true a DNA test would be taken to see if my husband was really the father or not. She became livid when I said that.

We didn't even live in Adelanto for a full week and we were in a major car accident on 395 and Air Expressway. We were sitting at a red light waiting to make a left turn and were hit from behind, I tried to avoid hitting the car in front of me so I swerved to the left and ended up hitting a pole. Our Ford Explorer was destroyed. A driver was on her phone and she wasn't paying attention and plowed through us like a bowling ball. Our second oldest was taken by ambulance to the hospital and I just had an abortion so they wanted to check my bleeding. I called my dad and told him what happened but he was out of state so my Nana met us at the hospital. Thank God all of us were okay. We ended up on the front page of the newspaper the next morning.

Levi already didn't really want to move to the high desert in the first place, but now he really hated it because we didn't have a car. It was an hour walk to and from the store. I was still working in San Bernardino at the time so I would ride down the hill with my Nana and meet my dad and he would drive me to work and then pick me up. My dad and my Nana got together and got us an Expedition that was a blessing. Not having a car with six kids was really hard and frustrating but God always made sure that our needs were met.

One day I was at work and I reached out to my first love's mom. I hadn't seen or heard from him in a while. She gave me his number and we talked for like an hour. He told me he was coming out here to see his first baby mama and he would stop by to see me. I was nervous and excited all at the same time. I knew I had to tread lightly because I was a married woman now. I couldn't throw myself at him like I wanted to. I had to actually keep it classy.

We exchanged emails and instead of making a lot of calls we emailed each other. The day came and he came to see me. He called me and said that he was in front of my job. I was rushing down the stairs so fast I almost fell on my face. We were right in front of my job talking and hugging. I didn't care who saw. He told me he lived in Vegas and I should come visit. To be honest I really wanted to because nobody could sling dick the way he could, or make me feel the way he could but I was married and I knew I would cheat so I never did. I didn't know at the time that he wanted me to bring the kids and come live with him. I thought he just wanted me to come and visit. If I would have known what his full intentions were, I would have filed for an annulment and taken the kids and moved to Vegas with him.

All I ever wanted was to be with my first love, however, it seemed like every time we were able to be with each other I was always in another commitment with Levi. This was a big commitment so I couldn't be a cheater. Especially not while I was married. I had the title and I had to play my role the right way. Not only that when we got married, we became one.

I ended up blocking him from my emails. This was the hardest thing for me to do because my heart belonged to him. But we were emailing a lot and Levi started going through my phone. I didn't want to get caught up so I ended it before it even began. I wanted him so bad but I was married so I had to honor that. Once again, he was single and I had already made another commitment. Why did this have to keep happening? I was married now so we would never have the opportunity to be together again, so I thought.

CHAPTER 18

My aunt, grandma, great aunt and great grandma would have girls time and since I lived in the high desert they would invite me to come. I would get really excited because of the invites I was finally feeling like part of the family. But Levi wasn't happy about it at all. He said he didn't move to the high desert for me to hang out with my family. He could have stayed in San Bernardino with his. So I wouldn't go because I didn't want to make him feel any type of way.

One night they called and said mother wanted to see me. I told them I would try and come. Well when I told Levi his response was the same. I was so mad all the years he would chill with his family and I didn't complain this was bullshit. The next morning, I got a phone call and she was dead. I was heartbroken and I felt so guilty. I vowed that if I ever had a daughter her middle name would be Ruby.

For a while Levis and I marriage was on good terms. I was working and he was working as well. Our two older sons played football so we would get up early on Saturday mornings to take them to their football games. He would always play the song let the bodies hit the floor as hype music. The boys would be super hyped. My only complaint about the games was that he would spend most of the time in the parking lot getting drunk, instead of watching our kid's game.

One day I was driving home from work and I stopped in the middle of the street. I started crying hysterically, I had a flashback of a time that my oldest two and I stayed in a transitional house for women and children. At that time Levi and I hated each other. I made sure he knew where his kids were but he didn't care, he wouldn't call to check on them or come to see them. But all I could do is thank God because he delivered us from the situation. We now live in a nice home; have two cars and I have a good job. I was so thankful and in awww of God.

I continued to reach out to Allison to get his daughters but it was starting to become a frustration. She didn't understand that my children had their own schedule and she thought that I was supposed to jump because she said jump. That's not how it works, I would bend over backwards to fit them in our schedule however sometimes it just didn't work out. Instead of her understanding that, she would talk bad about me and throw me under the bus saying I was trying to keep him from his kids. Little did she know that I would get into several arguments with Levi because he didn't want to get his daughter most of the time and I was still trying to get them.

Allison would continue to tell me that she was pregnant by my husband and since his cousin told us she was sleeping with his little brother; I would tell her to figure out who her baby daddy was and stop blaming my husband. She said, "At least my kids don't belong to my dad". I was like, what the hell are you talking about?" She said, "I was at your mother-in law house and your husband told all of us. He knew you were sleeping with your dad that your mom told him and that's why some of your boys look like him." I was like, "That's disgusting and I can't believe he said that." I said, "Y'all can believe what y'all want but I know it's not true."

FRANCES DUPREE

I hated the fact that when my husband was angry, he would bad mouth me. That's not what you do. He was supposed to be my covering my husband; he wasn't supposed to tell lies on me because he was angry. Every time she and I had an argument I would find out something that he said or did behind my back.

I called my mom and I asked her if she told my husband that I was sleeping with my dad? She got so angry and said that he was a bitch and that she wanted him to say that bullshit to her face. That I should have never married him and when she saw him, she was going to punch his lying ass in the face. She said as a matter of fact put that bitch on the phone. I told her I wasn't with him at the time.

A few weeks later I was so sick that I wasn't getting out of the bed and I didn't go to work. This wasn't normal for me; I always went to work no matter what. After two days my bosses started calling. I was too sick to even talk on the phone. I told my boss I was sick and he said my husband should have called and let them know something.

We went down to San Bernardino and went to urgent care. On the drive down Levi looked at me and said, "You're probably pregnant." I said, "Yeah right." We have six kids don't need or want anymore. I got to urgent care and I was pregnant I was so mad and I started to cry. I didn't want any more kids. Six was enough it was hard enough taking care of them. I called my sister from church and told her that I was pregnant and I was going to go the following day and get an abortion. Of course, she tried to talk me out of it and she also backed everything she said up with scripture. I ended up feeling like a murderer but I didn't want any more kids.

The next day I went to Planned Parenthood and was going to get an abortion. When the nurse did the ultrasound, we both said that's a big baby. The doctor came in and said, "You are five months pregnant." That I could have an abortion but it would be a two-day procedure. I laughed and walked out and called my husband and said were having a baby. God has a funny way of allowing things to happen because there was no way I was going to have a two-day procedure.

Even though I really didn't want another baby there was no way I was going to have a two-day procedure abortion. I wasn't happy at all, all of my kids were walking and talking and out of diapers and now I would have to start all over again. How did this even happen for six years I didn't get pregnant. Why now? I just started working at a law office close to my house. I was so mad and I felt like I was put in a no-win situation.

We ended up getting evicted from the house. The property management wasn't fixing things in the house like they were supposed to so I didn't pay the rent. When I got the paperwork, my co-worker helped me complete the response. When we went to court, I didn't know I was supposed to keep the receipts so when the judge asked for them, I didn't have them. We had to move in two weeks so we ended up getting a hotel.

I found a four-bedroom house but it wouldn't be vacant until the first and I was trying to move right away. But for some reason I kept going back to that house. We got approved for the house but I didn't have all the move in money. My boss gave me an advance on my pay. I hadn't been working there long so I was really surprised but I knew it was nothing but favor. My church also helped with the move in fees.

Mind you I never saw the inside of the house and I had already paid her the deposit. When we went to meet her on the first. Levi was with me so I was praying and praying because he was talking crap and I knew if he didn't like the house, I would never hear the end of it. When we walked in, I took a deep breath and we loved the house.

The cool thing was that the elementary school and junior high school was right there on the corner. Luckily the kids were on a school break. So, while I was at work, I made the calls to change their school and the principal gave me a hard time. I went above her head and I called the school district and I made a complaint. The principal called me and told me that she was going to allow my children to attend her school. That the school district doesn't run her school she does and I shouldn't have called them.

On the boys first day I went to pick them up and I was at the gate for the fifth graders. I heard this teacher talking to another teacher about a new kid in his class that he was a perfect kid the first half of the day but the second half terrible. I mean this teacher talked so bad about this little boy. I walked up to him and introduced myself well he was talking about Tristan the whole time. I told him that he shouldn't talk that loud about students you never know who's listening. I said, "The next time you have a problem with my kid, call me and don't gossip about him to your teacher friends."`

This teacher would continue to complain about Tristan. I had a meeting with the principal and she wanted to demote him. I told her that was the stupidest thing I ever heard of. That he passed the fifth grade with flying colors why you would put him back for his mind to not grow for a whole year. I started making it a point to pop up on Tristan because I wanted to catch him in action.

The first time I went my son was doing his work, other kids were on their phone and the teacher had his feet on the desk on his phone. I went off I told the teacher that he had the nerve to talk all this crap about my kid and he's the only one working but these kids are acting a fool and it's okay. I said you better not ever call me about my kid again.

This was just the beginning of my problems with this school. Tristan got his act together because he never knew when I was gonna pop up. My fourth son Kendrick started acting a complete fool. He would lose his temper and try to run away from the school. In the after-school program he destroyed the whole class room flipping over desks and throwing everything everywhere. He even broke the teacher's glasses. I would get pictures from the after-school coordinator of Kendrick standing on top of buildings. It got so bad his teacher and the whole class was scared of him after he kicked a classmate in the back and destroyed the classroom. After an IEP assessment we learned that he had ADHD and Attention Deficit Disorder.

I would drop the boys off early to school on my way to work. One day I got a call an hour after being at work telling me Mason was being suspended from school. I was in shock because he was one of the ones that never got in trouble at school. The principal told me that Mason socked a second. I said that sounds completely out of his character. She said that Kendrick took the second graders quarter and the second grader slammed Kendrick head on the concrete. That she was so scared for her second grader I said and what about my first grader? Kendrick went off when he found out Mason got in trouble the principal grabbed him so hard her nails made holes in his shirt.

I called the school district and the police. The police came to my house and took the report, took pictures of Kendrick's shirt and informed me that it would be hard for charges to be pressed on her because she was the principal and it would take several reports for a DA to even look into the case. I became really angry and told her that just because she has a title doesn't give her the right to treat my son like that.

Levi called me and said that CPS came to the door. I asked him a million questions and he had no answers for me. He gave me the workers number off the card and I blew her phone up. I took the kids to see her the next day I wasn't playing. After all the interviews she said she was closing the case. The reason I knew it was the principal is because of the time line she told me that she got the calls and how frequent they were.

This was a really hard experience for me because I started having flash backs of my childhood. I was seven when I got taken from my mom, and my mom was seven when she entered the foster system. I wasn't a bad mom and I would be damned if I lost my kids. But I had favor throughout the whole situation because I wasn't a bad mother and I wasn't doing anything wrong, there was no reason for the call and especially no reason for my children to be taken. That night while I was in the shower, I cried my soul out and just kept thanking God, that the generational curse had been broken.

I had my mom come out to help because I was going to have my baby soon. I should have known better. We didn't have the best relationship but when I called, she always came to my rescue. We didn't really know our neighbors but she was in the neighbor across the street backyard getting high. I was so pissed I told her I don't associate with my neighbors. "We're not in the hood and that's not what I brought her out here for". She was on her period and going through a roll of toilet paper a day. I told her she couldn't do that and when I buy toilet paper that it last for months. We were all going to my doctor's appointment and she got in the front seat this made Levi mad because that was his seat. I asked her to move and she was pissed.

I told her when you're married your husband comes first and she had to sit in the back. This made her mad even more. When I got to the doctor, I begged the nurse practitioner to help me go into labor because I was miserable and my back was killing me. She shoved her hand up there and told me to go straight to the hospital. While I was at my appointment my mom and Levi were getting drunk in the car. They dropped me off at the hospital and went home.

I called my aunt and told her I was in the hospital and I was starving. She snuck me a burrito in and it was bomb. She said she had to leave at 4 am to take my little cousin to school. I refused the epidural but after so many hours those contractions were starting to come super strong and I was begging for it but it was too late. Paceson came right before my aunt had to leave.

MARRYING OUTSIDE OF GOD'S WILL

At five in the morning I got a call from Levi asking me where the fuck I was at. I told him I just had our son. He swore he didn't remember dropping me off. At this time, he worked at Walmart so on his way to work he stopped by to see me and the baby. We decided to name him Paceson Rion Lockwood. No one knew I had the baby I looked on Facebook and my mom had posted about me being in the hospital. I was so mad. I told her when we were ready, we would post that I had the baby that it wasn't her place.

I got discharged on Sunday. When I got home, I took my baby straight in the room. My mom felt some type of way because I didn't let her hold him right away. When I finally did, I told her not to take pictures of him because I didn't want him all over the internet. This was the last straw for her and she wanted me to drop her off at the train. I did just that with no hesitation.

CHAPTER 19

I went back to work first thing Monday morning. I had put in enough over time hours so I was only working part time. I admit having the baby in the office was a big distraction and I started making a lot of mistakes. I almost lost my job. Not too long after I found out that I was pregnant again. This time it was early enough and I went straight to have an abortion. I just had a baby and I definitely didn't want another one.

One day I was at work and something told me to sign on Levis Facebook. He was messaging some chick by the name of Avery. He didn't know I was on his page and I saw a glimpse of their conversation. He told her to call him right now and she said okay babe. I made up an excuse and I flew home running every red light and stop sign. When I walked in the house he was in our room on the phone. I snatched the phone away from him and I threw it on the floor.

His brother ran in the room to see what all the commotion was about and I threw my heel over his head and hit Levi. I told his brother that I caught this bitch cheating again. I told Levi to get his shit and to get the fuck out of my house. I threw most of

MARRYING OUTSIDE OF GOD'S WILL

his clothes in the front yard and he started walking down the street. I hopped in the truck and drove on the side of him and I was cussing him out.

Later that night he came home and apologized and of course I forgave him. But that morning I checked his phone and she was messaging him all night. I made it a point to remember her name and I inboxed her. When she replied she was very nasty to me. She said he told her I was gonna try and break them up. I asked her why she wanted a married man with eleven kids who worked at Walmart.

Avery said I couldn't tell her about her man. That she knows he has a good job that pays all my rent and bills. That he just bought me a BMW and he's going to continue to sleep downstairs until he's able to transfer his job and be with her. That he told her he wanted another daughter and I could only have sons and I was jealous of his daughters. This really broke my heart because I wanted a daughter so bad and couldn't have one. But why would he tell her all of this? He didn't really love me or he wouldn't be doing the things that he was doing.

Now I was pissed and I told her she was full of shit. I said, "Screenshot the messages and send them to me." and she did. Everything she said was true. So, I decided to tell her the truth. I told her we live in a single-story house took a picture covered my address and sent it to her. I took a picture of his paystub and sent it to her. She called me and his little brother got on the phone and told her his brother was lying to her. But she swore he was lying to her because I was standing right there. She said she knew his family so I told her to contact his brothers. I even gave her the number to Apple Valley Walmart. She called Walmart and then Levi called me and he was livid. He said she kept blowing up his job phone and got him in trouble. I went off, "How dare you talk shit to me for exposing you and you're cheating". We argued all night.

The next morning, I woke up so broken and I called my

sister and told her what was going on. I told her I was gonna take the kids and move with my dad in Lake Havasu. She asked me to just go to church with her. I looked a hot mess but I went. I left the kids at home because I knew I was going to break down and I didn't want them to see me that way. I tried to stay in the background but the pastor was on me.

He asked me if he knew me from Walmart and I said, "No." He preached the house down and he prophesied into my life. I broke down and cried my heart out. After, I felt better. I went to pick Levi up and he looked like crap. I asked him what was wrong and he told me all day that he heard me in his head crying. That it broke his heart. I told him about church and I told him he should go whenever he had a Sunday off.

A few weeks passed and he was acting really funny one night. He took my phone and he went outside and literally disappeared. His brother and I were walking around outside looking for him. I walked to the back of the house where the desert was and I saw a car slowly approaching and I thought it was him so I ran up to it. A guy hopped out and pulled a gun on me. I apologized to him and he got in the car and left.

When the car drove back past my house the guy got out and started talking to me. I had my son's tablet and logged on to Levis' account and I saw that he and Avery made plans for her to pick him up. So I stayed outside for like two hours talking to the guy. We exchanged numbers and I used my son's phone and we talked all night. He even offered to help Levi's little brother the next day while I went to work but Justice refused his help. I hadn't heard from Levi all night or all morning.

After lunch when I got to my desk, he started blowing up the office phone. My co-workers ended up telling him I left for the day so he could stop calling. When I got home I was every hoe and bitch in the book because he saw the messages and he knew I stayed outside talking to the guy. I was like you out cheating with some chick and you mad because I had a conversation with someone I met looking for you. I grabbed my kids and went to stay at my friend's house.

On my way to my friend's house I met Levi's cousin at the gas station. She said that she needed to tell me something really important on the phone. When I got out she hugged me and started crying. She told me that she and her girlfriend were in the room. Levi was drunk and came in the room and told them to let him watch them have sex. I apologized to her and I felt so bad. I always let her stay with us whenever she needed no matter where we lived. She said that wasn't the first time he came at her like that.

I told her that I left him and was going to stay with my friends. I told her not to go back to the house by herself. She said she was waiting for her mom to get off work to go to my house and get her stuff. She said I should have left him a long time ago. I told her I loved her and if she ever needed me to just call.

I stayed at my friends for like three days. I got a call at work from one of the boys baseball team moms asking if Levi was ok. I said as far as I knew, yes. She said he wrote a post on Facebook talking about killing himself. This was very concerning to her and she was sending the police to my house. I said, "Ok". I knew that he did this for attention and he wanted someone to tell me so I could run back home to him. I left work and went to get my kids from school. My house was at the corner. I saw a weird car in my driveway and then I saw his baby mama Allison walk out of my house.

I got my kids and walked down the street and went into my house. When I walked in it was a gathering in my house. His god brother started talking crap to me calling me the devil. I asked him if he knew Levi scared his little cousin off. That she said he was drunk and asked her to watch her and her girlfriend have sex? He called me a liar. I tried to call her but she didn't answer. His brother Joshua said he heard about it but he didn't believe it. His cousin told me till this day that his brothers didn't believe her.

I told Allison she wasn't welcome in my house and slammed the door in her face. Everyone was on my head because he posted about killing himself. He admitted to doing that to try and get my attention and get me to come home. Allison called the police because she assumed from the divorce papers I wasn't allowed to be at my own home but that wasn't the case. I ended up having the police tell her to get off my property.

Allison was Levi's brother Joshua's ride and he was trying to take Levi down the hill with him but he wouldn't go. Joshua was really upset and said they just lost their grandma and he couldn't deal with losing a brother too. Levi said he wasn't going to kill himself. The whole time he was super quiet and not saying much. His god brother kept saying before I came Levi was being himself but once I got there, he was quiet and acting like a bitch. He told him that he needed to leave me and file for custody of the kids and he told him no and I put him out of my house. I ended up coming back home and trying to work it out.

That weekend we were on the football field watching the boy's game and Avery called my phone. She told me that she paid for them a room and picked him up. She didn't want my nasty ass husband that he fucked her and ate her pussy and I could have him. That they didn't use a condom so she would let me know in a few weeks if she was pregnant or not. I told her she was a nasty ass bitch and to stop calling my phone.

He was sitting right next to me and said I needed to block her because he thought we were past this. That bitch was lying she was mad because he didn't fuck her. I looked him dead in the face and said if she is pregnant, we were done for good. He yelled at me, "You stupid bitch she is miserable and you're gonna be miserable with her" and he walked home. All the parents that were in ear shot were staring at me. It was so embarrassing.

MARRYING OUTSIDE OF GOD'S WILL

A few weeks later she called me and said she wasn't pregnant and I didn't have to worry about her anymore. To tell my husband to stop calling her and to stay out of her inbox. During this going on we had to move and it was getting down to the wire of us only having a few days to move.

CHAPTER 20

My mother in law called me and asked could she come stay with me. I told her I didn't mind but I had to discuss it with Levi. I called him and said, "You need to be glad I have a heart of God". He said, "Why"? I said" Because your mom needs to come stay with us but remember the last time the kids and I stayed with her she put us out after I got out of jail?". I said, "We used to sleep in the car at the park and I would wash them up with baby wipes. They would go to school and I would go to work."

Sometimes we would go look at a house and that night go back and sleep in the car in the driveway. One night I was so tired but I was trying to stay up because we were in a driveway and I saw an angel that turned its head at me like it was okay for me to go to sleep. That it would watch over us. I slept so good it felt like I slept for days but really I only slept for four hours.

I thank God though that isn't our life anymore. Levi said where I was, I said with Allison that's where you go every time things get bad. You didn't stick it out with us. God kept closing doors on me until I dealt with the past. It was the biggest blessing, I didn't see it at the time but I do now. I said I'll never forget

MARRYING OUTSIDE OF GOD'S WILL

how every time I would get a job, I would get fired because of a five year old warrant. Even a probation officer called me and told me to turn myself in but if he caught me it would be bad.

You went with me Levi don't act like you forgot. I went to court and they took me to jail. I was in custody at court. The judge asked where I was for the past five years, I said having kids I didn't have time to get in trouble. He asked if I had been to prison and I said no. The judge said he didn't believe me and was going to run a full background check on me. They gave me another court date like twenty days out. I went back to court you were there the public defender came and offered me a year in prison and I said, "No go back and talk to the DA."

I started praying and said, "Lord you hold the judge's heart in your right hand and can turn it any way you choose. You said those that trust in you wouldn't be ashamed so I trusted you and turned myself in". The public defender came back and said, "Time served, dismissed." I had a panic attack and couldn't breathe. "Now I know you didn't forget that Levi" he said, No I didn't because I told the police to check on you."

Levi said my mom got other kids she doesn't have to stay with us if you don't want her to. I said I wasn't made that way she can come stay and I'm going to make sure she feels at home. God doesn't give me what I deserve so I'm not going to do anyone else like that either.

The property manager of the house called and told me to come meet him. That because I worked for a law office. He was giving me the house. Levi's mom had moved in by this time. We were all in the kitchen drinking and I asked her what happened. She gives me all the details. "Levi said you so fucking nosey" I said, "I sure am."

Levi's mom said her and his baby mama Allison got into a fist fight. The next morning, she came to stay with us. We were short on the move in money so I borrowed it from his mom but when I got paid that Friday, I paid her back. The house was two stories just beautiful with a den open kitchen and a nice size backyard. The master bedroom had a walk-in closet and a jacuzzi bathtub. I loved it. Little did I know that this move was the final move Levi and I would make together.

I found a furniture store on Facebook. They had really nice furniture and it was cheap. Every time I moved, I got rid of the old and started off with the new. We went to the furniture shop on bear valley and put a deposit on the furniture and picked a delivery date. The carpet was cream and I wanted burgundy furniture.

By this time, I had started going to Harvest Bible University at my church. I was learning so many things about the bible and God and I loved it. My two sisters and I would always stay after church in the parking lot and talk. Our pastor would always tell us it wasn't safe to do that and to go home but we didn't listen. One particular night I asked them to pray with me. I told them the day that our new furniture came Levi and I got into a fight. He was mad because I wouldn't have sex with him and he was telling me he could have any girl he wanted and all this crap.

I told them, "Paceson came in the room and was crying for him". He got mad and threw a pillow at him and my baby flew across the room. I blacked out and socked him so hard I knocked him out of his stance. He snatched me by my hair and was dragging me across the floor. All the kids were crying. Tristan got mad and started walking down the street. Tristan finally came in the house and I locked Levi out. He was hitting the windows and trying to kick in the door. He was yelling he was going to kill everyone in the house. The kids were super scared. The kids were crying and saying they wanted to leave because they believed that their dad was going to really kill us. They were like hell naw. They asked me several times if I was sure that I wanted them to pray for me and I said, "Yes" they said, "Ok your whole life is going to change are you sure?" and I said, "Yes".

MARRYING OUTSIDE OF GOD'S WILL

They prayed with me and I felt a weight lifted off my shoulders. I had to rush home though because Levi was blowing me up. When I got home I got cussed out because I took too long to come home and he knew my fake class didn't last that long. Things between Levi and I started getting really bad. He would cuss me out all the time for no reason. My name was bitch all day every day.

One night we were in the room arguing because he wanted sex and I kept telling him no. Kendrick poked his head in our door and said leave my mom alone or we gonna catch a fade. I told Kendrick to close the door and go to bed. I had sex with him because I didn't want the other kids waking up. I just laid there so disgusted and I kept asking if he was done yet could he hurry up.

Our second oldest birthday came around and I planned a big surprise party for him. I invited everyone over and one of the ladies from the church made his cake homemade. I made a new friend from when our sons ran track together so I invited her and her kids as well. She was so awesome she came and helped me with organizing things and the clean-up part. I didn't know at the time that Camille and I would become great friends, even family.

Our oldest son was a little hater and he said Mason always had the best parties and he wanted the same kind of party when his birthday came and I said okay. That night Levi and I argued all night. I was so miserable. At this point every time he saw me, he was cussing me out for no reason. I would pray and pray and ask God why what did I do that was so wrong to deserve this?

I used to tell Levi's little brother that I was going to leave but I didn't want to because I knew the house was going to fall. He used to always tell me to do what I needed to do. I would take the kids to school, drop them off, cry and pray until I got to work. Wash my face as if nothing happened, try to stay at work as long as I could and cry and pray all the way home. I thought about killing myself a few times but I knew I was all my kids had.

I would take the boys to practice and leave him at home so I could have peace. A few times he found his way to the field and he would walk up and cuss me out. The other parents would look and stare. I was so embarrassed. I was on the field one day talking to my aunt about leaving him but I didn't want to leave the house. She said I hadn't had enough yet. I told her I promised the boys they wouldn't be homeless again. She told me about some resources and shelters but I didn't want them in a shelter.

That day finally came and I couldn't take it anymore. I told the kids to pack some stuff and we were leaving. I was holding Richy and I was in the hallway upstairs and Levi looked at me and said I better not ever come back because if I did, he would kill me in our room and no one would ever know. This spooked me to my core. He followed me outside to the car. It was nothing but God that I was able to maneuver around him, get in the car and lock the door and pull off. He was holding on to the door but I kept driving until he eventually let go.

CHAPTER 21

I called a friend of mine and I asked her if I could stay with her and she said yes. I'd say about two weeks we stayed with her. Then I was told one of my church members had an extra room in her apartment. I called and asked her if the kids and I could stay with her and she said yes. She welcomed us with open arms. Our oldest son broke his growth plate at a football game and he was on crutches.

His birthday was around the corner and he wanted to go to Johns and to have a party. I told him the party wasn't a good idea because his dad and I weren't together and it wasn't going to turn out the right way because I wasn't planning it. He didn't listen. At this point Levi and I were on speaking terms. The school kids would stay with him every other week because the house was literally around the corner from there school.

We went to Johns for our son's birthday and we didn't really speak to each other. The day of the party came. Not as many people showed up and Levi was pissy drunk. I was ready to leave so we sang happy birthday and he embarrassed our son and his brother was hyping him up. My friend from church and her daughter that I was staying with and her and everyone else that were with us left. I kissed my son and told him I loved him and took off.

Not even an hour later my mother-in-law calls telling me to come and get my kids, that Levi was going crazy and fighting all of her sons. He put a whole in every door of the house then he head-butted one of his brothers and fought the other. I called his brother Jaxon and told him I was coming to get my kids. He said no that he had it under control and Levi started tripping because I left. I said what he thought was going to happen that I wasn't living there before and I wasn't going to start now.

I found out the rules at the county changed and that I could apply for homeless again and I did. I thanked my friend for letting us stay but we needed our own space. We started staying in a hotel. At this time the engine in my suburban went out. I would walk to work but one of my mothers in the church would pick the kids up and take them to daycare. My daycare provider would take them to school and pick them up. She would pick me up after work and give us a ride to the hotel.

Tristan called my dad and asked if he could pay to get the truck fixed. That he was on crutches and it was really hard on us. My dad sent the money with no hesitation. Despite all of my screw-ups or anything that we went through in the past, my dad was always there for the boys and I when we needed him.

Halloween came around and my friend from church that made the kids cake invited us to go trick or treating with her and her kids. She made homemade chili and we had lots of laughs and went trick or treating. Levi called me because he wanted the kids and I told him no. That I tried to call earlier he didn't answer and we were already trick or treating. He said it's because of stupid bitches like me kids grow up without a dad. I hung up in his face and enjoyed the night with my kids. The kids and I were staying at the park hotel. I was paying for it because the county assistance only was for fourteen day.

I called Levi and told him that Thanksgiving was coming up

MARRYING OUTSIDE OF GOD'S WILL

and would he would like the kids and he told me no. I asked him if he was sure and he said, "Be a mom to your fucking kids bitch". And hung up in my face. We spent Thanksgiving with my friend. She cooked a big meal, Levi called and said he wanted the boys. I told him that I made other plans that I wasn't bringing them because he previously told me no. He hung up in my face.

One Sunday my sisters announced in church they were going to a conference in Atlanta. They said that God made a way for them to go. After church I told them I wanted to go. That they couldn't leave me behind. At this point I wasn't working Anymore. I had gotten fired on the first of the month. One night, Levi threatened to shoot up my hotel room and I told my coworker I wasn't coming in because I needed to get a restraining order against Levi. Well my coworker told my bosses and they said I couldn't come back to work until Levi was arrested. This was when I learned the hard way not to mix business with my personal life.

I called my dad and told him I really wanted to go to Atlanta and he paid for my ticket. I called Levi and told him I was leaving for the weekend and he needed to watch his kids while I was gone. I dropped the kids off to him and I left my truck with him in case of an emergency.

CHAPTER 22

My sisters and I were off to Atlanta. They already had a room all set up and I had a little money in my pocket. I was so thankful that God allowed me to share that experience with them. We got out there Friday evening. The revival was Saturday and the Evangelist knocked our socks off. She preached the house down. After we stayed for pictures and her book signing, a lot of the people there knew who my sisters were from the night we preached at the church for school.

THE EVANGELIST INVITED US TO GO TO CHURCH WITH HER THE next day but we told her we had to go home. God had other plans the airport was shut down for the first time ever. We went back and checked back in our room and changed our flight so we ended up staying for four or five days I believe.

LEVI WAS BLOWING UP MY PHONE. HE WAS UPSET BECAUSE WE HAD to stay longer. I asked him for a loan and he promised to send money but he never did. I was face-timing with our oldest son and Levi kicked in his door and snatched the phone out of his hands. I got a call later that Levi called all the kids downstairs and beat up Tristan in front of all the other kids. I Called, Levis brother Jaxon and I told him if his brother put his hands on my kids again, I would put him in jail.

I SENT THE EVANGELIST A FRIEND REQUEST ON FACEBOOK AND MY sister set up for us to have dinner with her. We were super excited to have dinner with her. When she finally got there, she told us that she had been pulled over and it was nothing but the devil because the whole time she lived out there she had never been pulled over. That she doesn't travel by herself but she had a word to deliver.

I WAS SURPRISED THAT THAT WORD WAS FOR ME. SHE SAID WHEN she accepted my friend request, she started looking through my page and that she saw a murder-suicide. She saw Levi killing me and then the kids and killing himself. I started to cry because I never told anyone that he used to threaten to kill me and the kids and then kill himself. We were talking and I started to tell her I always wanted a daughter but couldn't have one and didn't understand why God wouldn't give me one. I told her I had left him and that I was staying between their houses and I came because they couldn't leave me.

SHE SAID THAT I WOULD FIND LOVE AGAIN AND HE WOULD genuinely love me and accept all my kids. She said that he wouldn't have kids because there would be too many between us. She said I was going to have a daughter but I couldn't have one with Levi because out of spite he would have done something to her to hurt me. My mouth just dropped, how she could know all of this. I didn't tell her my life story and before the conference we had never met. That was nothing but God. We took pictures and tossed around the idea of me moving to Atlanta. Before we left, my sisters prayed for her and I did a covering prayer while they were praying. Till this day I swear the ground moved while we were praying.

THE NEXT DAY THE AIRPORT OPENED BACK UP AND WE FLEW HOME. I went straight to get my kids. I was so excited to see them. I missed them so much. What the evangelist said stuck in my mind. I couldn't stop thinking about it. I enjoyed my trip but after finding out what I did I felt guilty for leaving them. I also knew that the trip was necessary she really encouraged me.

CHAPTER 23

I officially moved in with my sister in Adelanto. It felt like we were having a sleepover every night. The boys that had school would continue to stay at their dad's during the week. I would buy groceries and send them over there. They were with me every weekend and my two little ones were mainly with me because they didn't have school.

We agreed that the boys would spend Christmas with him since I didn't have the money to do Christmas because I had spent it when I was paying for the hotel. Christmas Eve I took the kids over and Levi and I went to the Staters to buy Christmas dinner and we started arguing. I took him back home and took the kids with me but he wouldn't give me Paceson. His brother Justice said the kids shouldn't have to suffer because we were arguing. I took the kids and said, "No they don't".

At the time I was going between my sisters houses in Victorville and Adelanto. I went back to Adelanto and told her what was going on and she told me not to punish the kids. I took the kids back and Levi told me to keep my fucking kids that he was leaving with his brother Jaxon. His other brother

Justice said he didn't care he always spent Christmas with them and it wasn't going to change this year.

Levi said, "Don't keep them make that bitch be a mom and keep her own fucking kids. Don't watch them so that bitch can go and hoe the fuck around". I told them I would be back tomorrow evening to pick up my kids. Well the next morning came and I didn't feel right without my kids so I drove to the house.

Levi opened the door and he slammed the door in my face. The kids opened the door and Levi pushed them outside with me and locked the door. I told the boys I was sorry and I wasn't trying to start drama but it didn't feel right waking up Christmas morning without them. The boy's uncle Justice opened the door and told us to come in. Levi told him, "I don't want that bitch in my house and to put me out and I can take my fucking kids with me".

Justice got in his face and told him he was a bitch and that he was the big brother and Levi was the little brother. Justice pushed Levi out of the house. He said you cry all the time that you want her back but you treat her like shit that's why she left you in the first place. Their other brother came downstairs and asked what I was doing there and that I wasn't supposed to come until three. Levi didn't start tripping until I came around. The little brother Justice said I had every right to be there. The other brother Jaxon threw his hands up and said, "If they gone fight let them fight", and went back upstairs.

Levi said, "This bitch came over here causing all these fucken problems". Justice said, "You're the problem. Where are my nieces Christmas gifts? I get tired of having to lie for you that you got eleven kids stop acting like you only have eight". He said, "I'm going to beat your ass for making me get out of character in front of my nephews". Levi said, "I'm not going to fight you", and Justice locked him out of the house. The kids let him back in the house. He didn't say anything to me and we spent

MARRYING OUTSIDE OF GOD'S WILL

the whole day there. The plan was to take them with me but they wanted to stay.

New Year's Eve came and our church was bringing it in at a church in Apple Valley. I had the little kids with me and the older kids were with their dad. We got all dressed up and headed to the church. To my surprise Levi came walking in. He was dressed in pure white. He sat in the front with all the pastors and their wives. Levi came and took Richey out of my arms, he reeked of alcohol.

One of our members was singing and he went to the front with Richey and started dancing like he was in the club. I was so embarrassed and just put my head down. After he came and handed me Richey and sat right next to me. Our first lady was sitting on the other side of me. He started telling me how much he hated me and that he was going to fucken kill me.

Our first lady overheard him. She waved down her husband and when he came over she told him what Levi said and that he needed to move. Levi said we were lying and that he said that he loved me. But he got up and moved. First he sat in the back and he was mean mugging me the whole time. Then he sat on the opposite side. I ignored him as much as possible. After we ate and left, I was told by the first lady that the pastor picked up Levi and took him home.

That he was walking home from the church and fell in the middle of the street. On our way home my sister and I were talking about how bold that devil was. The next day was little Levi's birthday and he wanted to spend it with his uncle Justice and his dad. So I dropped him off at his dad's and they spent the day together.

CHAPTER 24

I ended up starting a business called Frances Contracting Services. I immediately started to advertise so I could build up my clientele. For a while business was booming. I was writing contract after contract. One morning, my sister was on the phone with her twin and they were talking about a townhouse in Apple Valley but she ended up not wanting it. I said well let me go see it y'all both have a place and I don't.

We went to see it, it was far from them and really surrounded by dirt. I hadn't lived in an apartment since I had four kids but the inside was nice. It was a small complex and I needed to take my kids home. Just like that we were in. I got the keys on my son Leo's birthday. I called Levi and told him I needed all of my TVs out of his house. I took the kids to go see it and they didn't much care for it because they were used to living in a house but I explained to them it was home.

I didn't move in right away because I needed to turn the utilities on. The kids stayed with their dad that night. Levi and I made plans to meet up. I was super horny and he was still my husband so I picked him up and drove to the junior high around the corner. We had sex in the truck in the parking lot and I dropped him back off.

I made it very clear to him that I wasn't going back to him that I just used him for his dick because he was still my husband. When I got back to my sister's house my brother was like don't be creeping around. When she got home from work that night, she told me my brother told her he thought I was sleeping with Levi. I told her I was using him for his dick and we laughed.

I was officially moved into our new place and it was so awkward because I haven't lived with just me and the kids in a long long time. I would get up in the morning drive the kids to school in Victorville, back home, and I drove back to get them. That became my daily routine. On the days my sister was off I would go to her house and stay there until they got out of school. Some nights they stayed with their dad so they wouldn't have to get up so early.

The biggest mistake I made was having sex with Levi because he was on my bumper now. He would blow my phone up all the time. At first, I didn't want him to know where I lived because I couldn't get what the evangelist said out of my head. But he made me feel sorry for him. He said that his family was taking advantage of him and just moved in. That they don't feed him or give him a ride to work. That every week when he gets paid, he leaves money on the counter for his little bro to pay the bills.

I was like how is a bill due every week and he said he didn't know. I told him he could spend a few days at my house and if he gave me gas, I would give him a ride to work. His job was on the way taking the kids to school. When the weekend came, I didn't even pick him up from work because he needed to go home. I was just trying to be helpful, I never said we were back together.

His family assumed that we secretly moved in together and

ended up moving out of the house. His lil brother Justice called and said on Tuesday that the lights would be off to tell Levi to get his stuff. I asked him what happened and he said that everyone was moving out. I told Levi and asked him what he was going to do because he couldn't live with me.

I had an older neighbor whom I really bonded with. She was older and had seven kid's six girls and a son. Her oldest daughter stayed in the apartments as well. I guess you could say I clung to her and I even started to call her mom. She would help me with the kids and cook for me. After I took the kids to school, I would be at her apartment every day. We did almost everything together. Grocery shopping, pray together, help each other make ends meet. On her worst days and my worst days, we were there for each other.

Eventually my neighbor talked me into letting him stay and giving him a chance but it didn't sit well with me. I told him he could stay long enough to get on his feet. He ended up getting a job in Apple Valley and I would take him back and forth but after a while I stopped. He was starting to get the wrong idea and I didn't like it.

It was Levi's daughter's birthday and she was my favorite. I reached out to Allison and asked her if we could come to the party. To my surprise she said yes. So, Levi the boys and I drove down the hill to the party. I sat on her couch and it brought back so many memories. Many years ago when I had two kids and I was pregnant with my third I had gotten out of jail. I was talking back and forth with my aunt. I was staying with Levis mom and would stay gone until the kids would fall asleep.

My aunt said we should come stay with her. My first love drove us up the hill and dropped me off at my aunts. Things didn't work out and my Nana brought us back down the hill well since I left and didn't say anything Levis mom said we couldn't stay with her we were gonna sleep in the park.

Levi called Allison and she said we could sleep in her kid's room because they didn't sleep in there. At this time Levi and I weren't together so he was sleeping in the room with her. But every time she would leave for work, we would have sex in the bathroom and the room I was sleeping in. So, it was weird being in her house again. I made it a point to apologize for the past before I left.

She and I ended up exchanging words because every time I got on my kids, she had something to say and it was pissing me off. I tried to keep my mouth closed because I wasn't trying to disrespect her house. Well she did it one last time and I had to get in her face and tell her when I'm talking to my kids don't say anything, she said they were her kids to and I told her they weren't and don't get crazy with me and I took my kids and left.

I took Levi down the hill to see his brother Joshua and I left him at his apartment. He kept calling me to come get him but I wouldn't. I didn't want him and I didn't want him staying at my house. We argued over every little thing and I was back to being his bitch. He had to go. My sister had invited me to the BET after party and I went with her.

I called his mom and asked her would she come up to watch the kids for me and she said, "Yes". I told her if her son wanted to see his kids while she was there, he could but he had to be gone by the time I got home. I also asked her not to tell Levi where I was going. I drove to my sister's house. We stopped by the mall and got on the freeway.

On our way down the hill I posted pictures and then Levi started blowing up my phone. Where was I going? I needed to hurry and get home. I was networking and giving out business cards. I took lots of pictures with different celebrities. My sister and brother-in-law and I had so much fun. While we were down there, Justice texted me and asked when I was going home, I said, "I didn't know". He said Levi was tripping and his mom wanted to leave. Well I didn't drive so I couldn't leave until my ride was ready.

I got home that night and Levi was asleep on my couch. I tapped him and told him he had to leave that he should have been gone. He got angry and got in my face and started cussing me out. He told me to drop him off. He was staying with someone in Apple Valley close to the hospital. I let him out by Toms and he snatched my phone out of my hand. I tried to chase him down but I couldn't catch him. I ended up just going home.

On the way taking his mom down the hill the next morning she told me that he flipped out on her and the kids got scared. That he kept questioning her where I went, she said, "She didn't know". She said that he was questioning the kids trying to find out if I was seeing anyone and what I have been doing. She said that around nine she told him to leave and he got in her face and started cussing her out and grabbed her by the throat.

She said the kids got in his face and told him not to mess with their grandma and then he got in their face too. She said that his brothers said they would catch a fade on sight when they see him for the way he disrespected her. She said she backed down and just let him stay. She didn't want him really going crazy in front of the kids. She told me that she didn't have a problem keeping the kids for me again but next time he can't come. I paid her and thanked her and dropped her off.

When I got up the hill, I kept calling my phone and he didn't answer. I called his phone and he kept cussing me out. I ended up calling the police and they called him and he gave me my phone back. But he had factory reset my phone and everything was gone. My sis kept telling me to send her the pictures and I was enjoying myself so much that I forgot. I was so pissed all my contacts were gone and everything was completely wiped clean from my phone.

CHAPTER 25

I started focusing on trying to build my business even more. I continued to advertise to people through social media. I would set appointments and some followed through and others didn't. I ran across Pastor Carter. He and I kept canceling on each other. I went to one of his Wednesday night services. Immediately he had my attention; he prayed before he did anything, he controlled the room. My oldest had the worst attitude and after Carter prayed his attitude changed quickly.

When I tell you that he preached the house down. Spirituality he had my nose wide open. I wasn't attracted to him physically but I was spiritually. We started messaging each other and got to the point where we were talking every day. I eventually ended up telling him I had a crush on him. After that the messages that he would send me I was surprised because he was a pastor.

He was single and had a daughter. He ended up opening a church in Palmdale and my nose was wide open when I had the gas the boys and I would go. Levi hacked my Facebook and sent him threatening messages. He also blocked the evangelist and I didn't understand why because he didn't even know who she was. Levi was starting to do weird things like popping up places he shouldn't.

I would talk to Carter about it and he would give me advice from time-to-time. Carter had to move out of his house in Apple Valley and he asked if he could stay with me. I told him it was ok. I felt like we needed a man around because Levi was being so weird. I gave him my room and I slept in the room with the kids. We were only friends so I didn't see the harm in it.

My older kids weren't having it and my oldest called him a fake pastor and fake prophet. The little ones took to him. He mostly stayed in the room but I would cook for him and tried to make sure he felt comfortable. One morning I took the boys to school and on the way home I saw Levi. I went next door and told mom she kept her door open but never saw him.

I went to my truck and it was a huge cardboard sign saying will you marry me. I was really freaking out because no one saw him come in the apartments or leave. I called Carter and told him what was going on but he never came outside. He said that Levi wasn't stupid enough to ty an come in the apartment and if he did he was going to show him what he was really working with. I took him down the hill to work. He promised me gas when he got paid. He ended up buying a Benz and he didn't pay me anything.

He was gone one day and my neighbor said he was fake and I needed to put him out. Even though she knew nothing was going on inside looking at the situation from the outside it didn't look good. My neighbor asked him for a word and he told her to go to church. Carter brought his daughter with him. I didn't know she was coming and his daughter's friend. The little girl stayed for almost a week. I didn't like it at all and started feeling like he was taking advantage of me. My dad was coming

MARRYING OUTSIDE OF GOD'S WILL

to visit and he had to go. I felt bad because I didn't give him a lot of notice but he had to go.

Carter's attitude was terrible while he was packing to leave. He didn't want to leave. He was being so rude to his daughter and didn't say anything to me or the kids. I thought he was ungrateful. I was so mad thinking about all the times I went to Palmdale to support him. I even accepted his invite to his birthday celebration/church ceremony. He stayed for almost a month, didn't help financially cook or clean and had the nerve to have an attitude when it was time to go. We stopped talking for a little while.

A few weeks passed and Carter texted me saying he wanted his friend back. I was surprised but we started to be cool again. My oldest didn't like that I was still in communication with him. He kept telling me he was fake. He texted me one night and said he wanted to make love to me, I said, "Well you never said anything, a closed mouth don't get fed."

CHAPTER 26

Kendrick got really sick and I took him to St. Marys. I called Justice and told him to tell his brother. Well Justice brought him up to the hospital. Somehow my purse ended up getting stolen and I didn't even have the key to my truck. Levi ended up staying to help me out. The next day we walked to the hospital and my friend loaned me money so I could get the truck rekeyed. Levi and I kept getting into it because he wanted sex and I didn't he swore I was fucking everyone in the high desert because I wouldn't fuck him.

Levi's God brother picked him up from my apartment and I begged him not to bring him back. To leave him down the hill. That morning when I woke up, I didn't see him so I was happy. I thought he was left down the hill. Well he was in the apartments talking to my neighbors so I hurried, packed up the kids and left because I didn't want him to try and come in.

My car smelled like smoke. My clothes were in the trunk because I had just done my laundry. I looked for something to wear and all my clothes were burned and had cigarette burns. It wasn't hard to put two and two together. Levi slept in my car and burned all of my clothes. This made me hate the smell of smoke.

My neighbor called and said he was trying to get in my house. I said, "If he breaks in call the cops." She called me back and said, "Bitch you didn't tell me he had a key." I said, "What the hell, how? Ur mom has my extra key and I have my key with me." Tristan checked his backpack and his key was missing. I told her he stole my son's key. She told me he left.

The next day her boyfriend changed my locks so I thought it was good. Well I left that night and she called me freaking out. I said, "What's wrong?" She told me that Levi was in my house on top of the kid's closet all morning and he told her word for word everything we talk about. How many times I left what I and the kids did all day.

I went first thing the next morning and got a temporary restraining order. I also filled full custody for the kids. On my way home I saw him sitting at the bus stop close to my house. I was on the phone with my neighbor and she said that she would serve him for me. We drove back to the bus stop, he started walking to the car and she served him. I didn't hear from him until I saw him at court for the hearing.

Mother's Day came and I was not in the mood. My neighbors' kids all got together to do a party for her and her daughter that lived there because they were moms. Her son came and got me out of my apartment so I could join in. I was hesitant at first but then I agreed. I started having so much fun. Then he walked in CT. He was her daughter's boyfriend's best friend. Of course, everyone started playing matchmaker. We talked for a little bit, flirted for a little bit and he asked me for my number. I gave it to him but my phone was off at the time. He ended up leaving and I walked him out. When we got to the drive way all the kids were outside. My oldest walked by and gave him a dirty look. If looks could kill he would be dead.

When I paid my bill, I called him and we started talking

every day. It felt kind of good knowing I still had it after the kids and the drama with Levi. We made plans to go on a date but he didn't call or show. When I finally heard from him, he had taken his meds, took a nap and overslept. We agreed to just leave it alone. He lived in Riverside, worked in the city of industry, and we just didn't think it was going to work.

The day of court came and I had my support system with me. My sister, my dad and a friend of mine all came to court with me. Levi came with his mom and his brother Justice. It was the first time I saw him in a few months it was weird. We were in one court and got switched to another courtroom. I was so nervous. I saw an attorney I knew and he gave me good advice in the hall.

Levi and I didn't talk the whole time. When we got in front of the judge he said, "Give her whatever she wants." I knew how the process worked and I didn't want the kids going to family court services. The judge said he was going to grant the restraining order for a year. Levi pleaded with the judge and told him he couldn't be away from his boys for a year. That it had already been months and it was killing him. That he had never been away from them for long. That he went to all of their award ceremonies, was at all their practices and all their games.

He said he was a very active parent. I agreed to every other weekend, holiday, school break, and birthday. I was also awarded full legal and full custody over the kids. I don't know why I was so nervous but I got everything that I wanted. My dad drove me home and he was pleased and said he was proud of me. Levi and I started to communicate again but it was mainly about the kids.

CHAPTER 27

In some weird way we were slowly becoming friends. He told me his troubles with his family and his baby mama Allison. I told him about Carter and CT. His brother would come and get the kids for him for his visits. Part of the agreement was his mom or Justice had to supervise his visits. The first visit came and his mom called me early that morning saying she didn't want to monitor for him and telling me how disrespectful he was.

He then called telling me how they were all against him and his mom would tease him and say if it wasn't for her he couldn't see his kids and he really wanted his relationship with his kids to work. I didn't ask for child support so from time to time he would send money for the kids. He was crying and saying he was really trying but his family was fighting against him. I felt bad for him of course.

After all the drama he was getting his kids when he was supposed to. Then Justice couldn't monitor because of work so Levi called my neighbor and asked her would she monitor for him and her and I discussed it and she agreed. My gala for school came and Levi and I were on good terms and he went with me. We had a lot of fun, my sisters and I had worked really hard for this. At this point on his weekends I would pick him up and he would stay at my house to visit the boys and on Sundays I would take him back home.

One day while taking the boys to football practice I grabbed my phone and I was trying to call my sister and see if she was home because I was going to hang out with her until their practice was over. Well my phone glitched and I called CT. I hung up as quickly as I could. He called me right back. I explained to him what happened and he didn't believe me and he laughed and we got caught up.

After that we started talking everyday again. The big day finally came for my graduation. It wasn't Levi's weekend but I asked him if we could switch weekends and he kept the kids for me. He agreed. I picked him up but when he got to my house he had been drinking and he started flipping out. Saying he was there the whole time I was in school that he should be able to watch me walk.

I told him that my dad was coming to take me to my graduation. My oldest said he didn't want to stay with his dad and I told him to get ready and he came with me. When my dad got there, I was rushing to leave and I had a bunch of stuff in my hand. While we were driving, I noticed my phone was missing. My son called it and we couldn't find it.

We checked Ross parking lot. It wasn't there I went back home and Levi was walking out the kitchen and my phone was on the counter. We finally got on the freeway to go down the hill. I was going through my phone and he had text Carter and I text him and apologized. He texted CT and I texted him and apologize to him too. CT text me back asking what I was up to and I told him on my way to my graduation.

Halfway to my graduation I got a call from my neighbor that Levi was outside cussing out Kendrick and hitting him so hard she said it looked like he was going to cave his chest in. I hung up on her and called and cussed him out. Then about twenty minutes later she called me back and said he was leaving and Paceson was crying for him grabbing him and he was pushing him in the house.

I told her I was going to come back and she said no that she was going to go get all the kids and watch them until I came back and I thanked her. She called me again and said that he let her get all the kids but Paceson and she heard all this noise in my house. The boys told him why did he break their mom door and he was in their face like he was going to fight them and she had to get in the middle. That was the last straw.

I called the police and told them what was going on. They told me to get home immediately. I called my dad to come get me, him and my son dropped me off and were gonna come back when the graduation started. I told everyone that I had to go. We took a few pictures. I showed them the pictures my neighbors sent of my house being destroyed.

As soon as I got in the car my neighbor who was like a mom to me called and she was crying. She said it was bad and she was going to try and get Paceson out of the house because she was scared for his life. My dad was flying on the freeway to get up the hill. He looked at me and said, "The police better get him before I do."

My neighbor called me back and put the police on the phone. I talked to the officer. I told him, "I trusted my neighbors with my kids that I was on my way." They said, "From what everyone was telling them he not only was a threat to the kids but also to everyone in the complex." As he was talking to me Levi poked his head out of the door and I heard the phone drop.

My neighbor picked it up and she said the police were running in my house with their guns out. Paceson was on the bed in the room downstairs and she was crying, begging the cops to let her get him and they said, "No". I was praying they didn't start shooting because bullets don't have a name on them.

They searched the whole apartment and they couldn't find him. By the time we made it to my apartment the police were still there waiting for me. They said they caught him and I had to walk to the car and identify him. He looked at me and put his head down. He said, "When you tell my family I'm in jail tell them you don't know who called the police." He put his head down and said he was sorry.

I felt bad for him. I didn't want to have to call the police on him but I felt like I didn't have a choice. When I finally walked in the apartment there were holes in most of my walls, my door to my room was kicked in, and liquids were coming out of my computer. My dad looked at me and apologized. I hugged all of my kids and just cried.

My oldest said he wished he was there because he would have fought him. I was glad he wasn't though because Levi would have hurt him, he always took his anger out on him when he was mad. Levi was blowing up my phone. I cussed him out. I dm'd his brothers so they knew he was in jail and I did as he said and told them I didn't know who called the police.

My dad left me with a couple hundred bucks so we got some shots. I was sitting at my neighbors and CT called me. It was midnight. He asked me was I sleepy and I said, "No why"? He said he was in Victorville and he wanted to come and see me and he congratulated me on my graduation. I went in the house took a shower and threw some clothes on.

When he pulled up I got in the car with him. We took some shots and we talked about his day. I told him about my day and we had a few laughs. He said he was gonna be in the high desert for the weekend and he owed me a date. He walked me to my door, hugged me, squeezed my butt and I kissed him on his cheek.

The next day Levi kept blowing me and my neighbor up. He asked me to bail him out and to give the bail bonds his brother's number. Which I did like a dummy. His brother kept asking who called the cops I kept saying I didn't know. I went and paid fifty. His mom signed for him. He told me not to talk to his brother anymore and when I told his brother and his brother said he was going to pick him up, beat his ass and bring him back to me.

I told his brother he wasn't welcome at my apartment anymore and after what he did, he wasn't going to see my kids for a while. CT met me at Olive Garden and we ate and laughed. We talked about his nephews and we talked about my kids. We both said what we were looking for in a relationship. The food was nasty but we had fun. He walked me to my car, gave me a hug and I kissed him on the cheek again.

The next morning, I went to the help center at the court and asked them to prepare my judgment for my divorce. I gave them all the orders including the orders for the restraining order. This was it we were really over there was no going back from this. Even though we would talk from time to time it was over. CT and I were talking everyday again either by text or phone call.

I invited him to the house. I dropped my kids off to their aunt in Adelanto because I didn't play about my kids. I wasn't that type of mom to have any man around my kids. Even though they met him before they didn't meet him in a way that had anything to do with me. I wasn't sure what we were doing yet and I didn't want my kids involved until we figured it out. My neighbor helped me move the kids upstairs and I moved downstairs. I actually got a bed and decorated my room real nice.

I was stressing on time so while I was in Adelanto my neighbor sister came in and cleaned the whole house for me. I got home fried chicken made rice and broccoli with cheese on it. I showered and put on a sexy bra and panties under my dress. When he got there, he brought a bottle of wine with him. We watched TV, talked, laughed, drank and ate.

He called his friend and told him he was staying the night with me. He said I owed him a massage he laid across my bed. I climbed on his butt and started rubbing his back. He said that I needed to do it naked. I took off my dress but kept on my bra and panties. I rubbed his back and then he started rubbing mine and took off my bra at the same time. He kissed me but I didn't like how he kissed so I didn't kiss him again.

He took his pants off and he had a porno penis I was a little nervous. He put on his condom and next thing you know he was putting it down. We had a real good time. After he went to sleep and I was up, the back door was open and I was nervous I didn't know if my crazy ex was lurking in the backyard. Also, I felt weird I hadn't spent the night with anyone except my husband for years. I was up all night while he was snoring.

The next morning, we did it again he tried to stick it in my butt but I wouldn't let him that was a line I didn't cross. He ate, I showered and I walked him out to his car. He hugged me and said he would call me. I kissed his cheek and he left. When I turned around my neighbor sister and mom were standing right there. All I could do was blush. He had told me not to tell them anything because they were basically family and he didn't want them looking at him funny. Of course, I couldn't hold water and told them everything that happened.

CHAPTER 28

I checked the mail and my divorce papers were there all I had to do was file them with the court. I looked up Levi brother Joshua's address in San Bernardino and filed my papers. All I had to do was wait for them in the mail.

ALMOST A MONTH PASSED AND I CALLED TO CHECK ON MY paperwork. They said there were two stacks on the desk but they had all been signed by the judge and I was officially divorced as of August 2, 2018. I was excited and sad all at the same time. I started to get really depressed not about Levi but because my marriage failed.

HOW COME HE WOULDN'T BE THE HUSBAND I NEEDED HIM TO BE? How come I wasn't strong enough to stay and fight for my marriage? Why wasn't I good enough to be genuinely loved? One night I drank a whole bottle of wine to myself and wrote notes to my kids and the police. My neighbor busted in out of nowhere and said she could feel the spirit something wasn't right.

WE CRIED AND PRAYED TOGETHER AND I RIPPED UP THE NOTES. I couldn't kill myself I had eight kids that were depending on me. They didn't have no one but me. I had to get it together. Through my business I ended up getting a job as a contract manager. It was going great. One day on my lunch Levi called me and I told him about CT and us sleeping together.

HE SAID WE WERE FINALLY EVEN AND NOW WE CAN GET BACK together and I told him he was crazy. He told me he got the divorce papers and he didn't care that I was still his wife no matter what. The kids were going to start school in three weeks. We always took them on a trip so I and my friend Camille picked six flags. Her three God sons spent the night with her. I picked up Levi and he went with us.

I PUT MAGIC MOUNTAIN IN MY GPS AND IT LITERALLY TOOK ME up a mountain. I was backing up and going forward Levi pushed my car so we didn't go over the cliff. We all had a great time. We didn't leave until it closed and we went to the water park and the regular park. I drove Levi home and he got emotional and started saying he wanted to come home. I made it very clear that it was never his home. I dropped him off and went home. I checked the mail the next day and my divorce papers were there.

A FEW WEEKS LATER I TOOK THE BOYS TO FOOTBALL PRACTICE AND my Facebook messenger went off. It was Momma Nikki I hadn't heard from her since I told her I was finally divorced. I eagerly read the message and stopped dead in my tracks. We're my sisters or brother playing a trick on me? This couldn't be real. I know it's not who it seems to be. I gave my number and said call me. Not even five minutes later my phone rang and I couldn't believe who I was talking to on the other end. It was my first love. He didn't know that I was divorced and he was reaching out to me because he happened to be single.

CHAPTER 29

*E*ven though I was disobedient and I married outside of Gods will he never took his hand off my life. God knew how much I could bear and there was always a ram in the bush when I needed it. I didn't realize the danger that I was putting myself and my children in by being disobedient. God always gives us free will, he will never force himself on us and in that aspect we have a choice. There's consequences behind every choice whether it is good or it is bad.

Even though I spent years trying to fill the void of love from my first love. I didn't realize until the calm after the storm that I was never alone and I was always loved because God was always right there with me from the start. That was Agape love and no matter how many wrong choices I made he never stopped loving me and he never left or forsaken me.

ACKNOWLEDGEMENTS

∽

I would like to acknowledge my sons for their unconditional love and respect for me through all of this although I wasn't always the mother that they needed me to be.

ABOUT THE AUTHOR

WEBSITE: WWW.GODS-WILL-MINISTRIES.COM

Frances Dupree is an emerging author and a woman of God that wears many hats. She is wife, mother, and supporter of her community and other women. She learned that her truth is worth telling to save souls. Through disobedience, she was exposed to many dangers such as depression, poverty, suicidal attempts, and physical and emotional abuse. God never took his hands off of her and he has blessed her to come out of it all victoriously.

❏

Made in the USA
Columbia, SC
05 April 2024